PRISON ETIQUETTE

Reproduction of original jacket design

PRISON ETIQUETTE
The Convict's Compendium of Useful Information

Edited and
with an Introduction by
HOLLEY CANTINE and DACHINE RAINER

With a Preface by
CHRISTOPHER ISHERWOOD

With Illustrations by
LOWELL NAEVE

With a New Foreword by
PHILIP METRES

Southern Illinois University Press
Carbondale and Edwardsville

Originally published 1950 by Retort Press
Southern Illinois University Press edition published 2001
Foreword copyright © 2001 by the Board of Trustees,
Southern Illinois University
All rights reserved
Printed in the United States of America
04 03 02 01   4 3 2 1

The publisher gratefully acknowledges the cooperation of Elmer Johnson in providing the text of *Prison Etiquette* that was used for the present edition.

The Danbury Story and *The Prison Theatre* have appeared, in considerably shorter versions, in the *Nation* and *Theatre Arts Monthly* respectively.

Library of Congress Cataloging-in-Publication Data
Prison etiquette : the convict's compendium of useful information / edited with an introduction by Holley Cantine and Dachine Rainer ; with a new foreword by Philip Metres ; with a preface by Christopher Isherwood ; illustrated by Lowell Naeve.
   p. cm.
  Includes bibliographical references.
  1. Prisons—United States. 2. Conscientious objectors—United States. 3. World War, 1939–1945—Conscientious objectors—United States. 4. Prisoners—United States. 5. Prisoners' writings, American. I. Cantine, Holley R. II. Rainer, Dachine.

HV9466 .P746 2001
365'.6—dc21
ISBN 0-8093-2375-3 (paper : alk. paper)   00-063516

The paper used in this publication meets the minimum requirements of American National Standard for Information Sciences—Permanence of Paper for Printed Library Materials, ANSI Z39.48-1992. ♾

Kuro-gane no	Watching
Mado ni sashi-iru	Through the iron-barred window
Hi no kage no	The sunbeams streaming
Utsuru wo mamori	Today
Kyo mo kurashitsu	Also I spent

SUGA KANNO

(Executed in Sugamo Prison, 1911 for participation in a plot to assasinate Japanese Emperor)

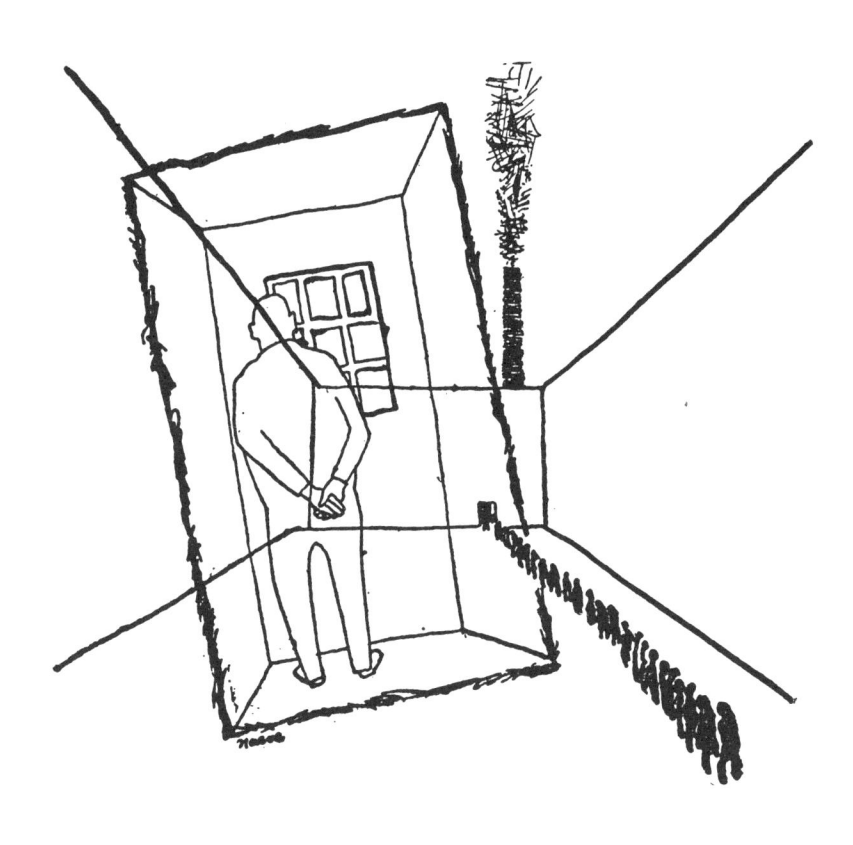

PRISON ETIQUETTE was hand-set and printed on a Gordon upright footpedal press by the Editors in an edition of 2000.

CONTENTS

Foreword: War Resistance and Radical Pacifism in the 1940s ix
Philip Metres

Preface xxix
Christopher Isherwood

Acknowledgments xxxiii

Introduction xxxv

SECTION ONE: RESISTANCE IN PRISON

Resistance in Prison 3
Clif Bennett

The Danbury Story 12
Howard Schoenfeld

A Field of Broken Stones (excerpt) 28
Lowell Naeve

The Ship That Never Hit Port 46
James Peck

SECTION TWO: THE PRISON COMMUNITY

Notes on My Life among the Dead Men in Denims 72
Curtis Zahn

NcNeil Island 86
Don Devault

Notes on the Prison Community 95
Bernard Phillips

SECTION THREE: ARTS AND LETTERS

The Prison Theatre 113
Roy Franklyn

Poems 118
Arthur Kassin, James Holmes, E. R. Karr, Lowell Naeve

Made-Work (story) 124
Sturge Steinert

Letter to a Penologist 132
William H. Kuenning

Letter 137
Jack Hewelike

FOREWORD

WAR RESISTANCE AND RADICAL PACIFISM IN THE 1940S

PHILIP METRES

FAULTY MEMORIES

Despite its historical distance, World War II still looms over the American cultural landscape. A glance at the current bestsellers or movies inevitably yields multiple representations of what Studs Terkel ironically referred to as "the Good War." World War II has become a paradigm for a just war, invoked whenever Congress debates U.S. military action against the dictator *du jour* (often yesterday's ally—Noriega, Hussein, et cetera). At the same time, it has become a nostalgic cultural myth of a country united by a common cause—even though such a characterization willfully forgets the racial segregation, the abject poverty of working classes, and the lamentable position of women in American society at the time.

The myth of the Good War also represses the dissent against the war, which was widespread until Pearl Harbor. But even after Pearl Harbor, and despite the compelling motives for U.S. involvement in World War II, an estimated fifty thousand Americans refused to fight, opting for conscientious objector status (for work in Civilian Public Service camps), noncombatant service in the armed forces, or confinement in a prison. Many had religious or pacifist convictions, though some objectors—the poet Robert Lowell, for example—argued that the Allied demand for unconditional surrender was tantamount to a betrayal of American principles. One anecdote about Lowell's internment serves to show the extent of American amnesia about dissent against the Good War.

In *Robert Lowell: A Biography,* Ian Hamilton recounts how, during the poet's arraignment on the charge of not registering for the draft, Lowell spent a few days in West Street Jail and happened to meet Death Row inmate Louis "Czar" Lepke. According to Jim Peck, a longtime antiwar activist, "Lowell was in a cell next to Lepke, you know, Murder Incorporated, and Lepke says to him: 'I'm in for killing. What are you in for?' 'Oh, I'm in for refusing to kill'" (Hamilton 91). Robert Lowell likely did meet Lepke. Lowell's 1950s poem "Memories of West Street and Lepke" recounts the poet's strange encounter with Murder Incorporated. However, Peck likely thought Hamilton wanted to know about Lowell Naeve, not Robert Lowell. Naeve, a fellow war resister who also passed through West Street Jail on his way to Danbury Prison, wrote a memoir, *A Field of Broken Stones* (1950), about *his* encounter with Lepke:

> Somewhere in the conversation we got around to the fact that I was in jail because I refused to kill people. The Murder, Inc., boss, who was headed for the electric chair, said: "It don't seem to me to make much sense that they put a man in jail for that." We looked at each other. There we were, both sitting in the same prison. The law covered both ends—one in for killing, the other in for refusing to kill. (29)

In Hamilton's biography, the little-known artist and anarchist Lowell Naeve has been erased and replaced by the literary giant Robert Lowell, whose memory of his "naïve" years in "Memories of West Street and Lepke" is the only canonical poem to emerge from the war resistance during World War II. Unfortunately, in "Memories," Robert Lowell casts himself as "a fire-breathing Catholic C. O." in the grips of mania and youthful rebellion and depicts other resisters as comic, insane, fey, or generally ineffectual. The Lowell/Naeve confusion illuminates some of the central difficulties with telling the story of war resistance during the Good War.

First, and most importantly, the erasure of Naeve is symptomatic of the absence of the activist from history. It has only been in the last twenty years that historians have questioned the "Great Man" historiographical paradigm by narrating what Howard Zinn calls "a people's history"—a history of dissent, not simply of dissenting intellectuals but of everyday people, often the most oppressed. In some current American high school texts, for example, the civil rights movement is discussed in the same chapter as the Kennedy presidency, as if Kennedy himself were the prime mover of those events. One of the great ironies of eliding Naeve is that he himself was an artist and writer whose personal anarchism led him to resist state power (both in the draft and in the prison) far more effectively than the revered poet, Robert Lowell. Still, Naeve's artistic output has gone largely unappreciated. At Indiana University, where I first discovered Naeve's work, his memoir had not been checked out in twenty years.

At the same time, this story also points to the possibility that literary canonization may enable war resistance to reach public consciousness where traditional modes of activism have failed. I learned about war resistance during World War II, for example, through Robert Lowell's famous poem, "Memories of West Street and Lepke." In the poem, Lowell recalls, "I was a fire-breathing Catholic C. O., / and made my manic statement, / telling off the state and president" (Lowell 91). Literature, supported and sustained by the academy and the marketplace, has cultural capital, to use John Guillory's phrase; in other words, literature is imbued with a certain authority that can empower and legitimize dissenting perspectives.

Lowell's canonical poem, however, shows that literary values can also distort history and delegitimize dissent. "Memories," upon closer reading, is a kind of public confession that actually denigrates the speaker's past refusal to serve in the war; it reflects, ironically, a midlife crisis during the hysterically anticommunist 1950s. Ultimately, the poem fails to represent, in any meaningful way, the breadth and complexity of resistance engaged in by war objectors (see "Confusing a Naïve Lowell and Lowell Naeve," *Contemporary Literature*, Winter 2000, for an in-depth treatment of Robert Lowell's poetry and war resistance).

The republication of *Prison Etiquette,* first published by two anarchists in 1950, Holley Cantine and Dachine Rainer, does not simply restore the soundtrack to Robert Lowell's deformed and silent images of war resisters, it writes another script. Among its various pieces by activists, *Prison Etiquette* includes the writing of two resisters who served alongside the poet in Danbury Prison, Lowell Naeve and Jim Peck. Both authors tell parts of the larger story of war resistance by conscientious objectors during World War II. But before discussing *Prison Etiquette* further, let us first consider the broader history of conscientious objection.

CONSCIENTIOUS OBJECTION IN THE UNITED STATES BEFORE WORLD WAR II

On June 8, 1789, James Madison submitted to the Continental Congress what would become Article II of the Bill of Rights, the article now used as the touchstone for the militia movement in the United States. This early draft contained a clause articulating the right of those individuals whose conscience impels them to refuse to fight in wars: "The right of the people to keep and bear arms shall not be infringed; a well-armed and well-regulated militia being the best security of a free country; *but no person religiously scrupulous of bearing arms shall be compelled to render military service in person*" (italics mine, Sibley and Jacob v). This clause was dropped before the Bill of Rights reached its final form. Part of the reason may have been that the volunteer status of the army precluded the necessity of conscription; only with the rise of modern warfare—in the United States, since World War I—did the question of conscientious objection to war resurface.

In their landmark history of war resistance, *Conscription of Conscience: Conscientious Objectors and the American State 1940–7,* Mulford Q. Sibley and Philip E. Jacob locate the origins of conscience in religious contexts; they argue that "during the first two and a half centuries of the Christian era, Christians were almost without exception conscientious objectors, not only because they objected to the shedding of blood, but also because service in the army was connected with worship of idols and sacrifices to the emperor" (1–2). In one famous case, Maximilian, the son of a soldier in the Roman army, refused to serve because he had recently converted to Christianity. According to historian Ronald Musto, "entreated by his father and the civilian governor, [Maximilian] replied, 'My army is the army of God, and I cannot fight for this world, I have already said it, I am a Christian.' For his declaration of loyalty he was condemned and executed" (43). The twelfth-century Albigensians and the sixteenth-century Anabaptists revived that early Christian tradition and directly influenced the development of conscientious objection as a legal category in the United States in 1940. After C. O.'s received only limited rights during World War I, when the United States sentenced 17 people to death and 142 to life imprisonment for refusing to serve, the Historic Peace Churches (Mennonites, Friends, and Brethren—all Anabaptist sects), along with political groups, fought for legislation that would recognize conscientious objection as a legal category.

The Selective Service and Training Act of 1940, Section 5 (g), allowed legal C. O. status and alternative service but did so by narrowly defining its status through religious, rather than philosophical or political, definition:

> Nothing contained in this act shall be construed to require any person to be subject to combatant training and service in the land or naval forces of the United States who, *by reason of religious training and belief,* is conscientiously opposed to participation in war in any form . . . or shall, if he is found to be conscientiously opposed to participation in such non-combatant service; in lieu of such induction, be assigned to work of national importance under civilian direction. (italics mine, Sibley and Jacob 487)

Congress refused to drop the religion stipulation, alleging that communists would take advantage of the revised act to evade military service. Those fears proved to be unfounded after Germany invaded the Soviet Union in 1939, and the Communist Party then framed the war as an antifascist struggle. In any case, C. O. status, as defined by Congress, ensured that nonreligious C. O.'s would be forced to go to prison rather than allowed to participate in the Civilian Public Service, also known as the C. P. S.

THE CIVILIAN PUBLIC SERVICE DURING WORLD WAR II

C. O.'s with religious support often chose alternative service in the Civilian Public Service camps established by the peace churches, in the hope that they could be a nonviolent witness while remaining loyal to their country. For Selective Service head General Hershey, the C. P. S. was an "experiment in democracy." For six years, almost twelve thousand men worked eight million days: fighting forest fires, battling soil erosion, building dams, planting six million trees, farming the land, raising money for war victims, working in mental hospitals, and volunteering as human guinea pigs for medical research on disease.

The objectors at the C. P. S. camps expressed a wide range of ideological and religious views; even a subgroup as united as the Mennonites exhibited a broad range of attitudes and beliefs. A short list of the various affiliations of objectors includes: Mennonites, Brethren, Friends (Quakers), and other Protestants, especially those influenced by the Social Gospel movement, Roman Catholics, Jehovah's Witnesses, Christadelphians, Seventh Day Adventists, Molokans, Black Moslems, Black Israelites, Hopi Indians, socialists, and anarchists. The problem of categorization becomes quite plain when considering whether these groups should be termed "pacifist." As absolute nonresistants, the Mennonites rejected the pacifist label, because for them it connoted a position that might advocate nonviolent resistance; at the other end of the spectrum, the Jehovah's Witnesses actively prepared for the final battle between Christ and Satan but refused to take part in state conflicts. The Social Actionists, who saw objection to war as part of a broader social vision, preferred the term "war resister" and left an indelible mark on C. P. S.

Unfortunately, as Sibley and Jacob document, "the conditions of alternative service were progressively restricted and the men assigned it in effect penalized for their beliefs" (11). The close cooperation of the government and the churches almost always resulted in more governmental restrictions than pacifist experimentation. As Gordon Zahn noted, in *Another Part of the War: The Camp Simon Story*, General Hershey stated before a congressional hearing that "the conscientious objector, by my theory, is best handled if no one hears of him" (80). As Hershey exerted more authority over the operations of the camps, the C. P. S. gradually came to resemble a branch of the military.

Consequently, many objectors came to believe that the C. P. S. experiment was a failure. No one received a cent from the government (living on eight cents per day funded by the peace churches), and many objectors were sorely underemployed or forced to do meaningless "made" work. While some continued to offer their witness in service, others protested, calling the whole program "involuntary servitude without pay . . . in violation of the 13th Amendment . . . [and] mirrored the global trend toward totalitarianism" (261–2). Protests included walk outs, work slowdowns, and work strikes, which inevitably led some C. O.'s in the C. P. S. to prison.

Sibley and Jacob relate the narratives of those objectors whose resistance to the war and to the state took on unsettling extremes; for them, "the story of conscientious objectors during World War II is incomplete without a treatment of what was known as 'absolutism'" (399). Corbett Bishop, the most dramatic and controversial of the absolutists, began his objection in a C. P. S. camp, but he soon walked out. Over the course of the next two years, while incarcerated or hospitalized, he fasted for 426 days and engaged in absolute resistance—he refused to eat, stand, dress himself, or go to the bathroom—for 337 days. Bishop articulated his absolute refusal as the spirit's essential freedom, despite how the body is disciplined: "the authorities have the power to seize my body; that is all they can do. My spirit will be free" (qtd. in Cooney 107). "Absolutism," despite its deeply problematic nature, cannot be categorized as purely negative. For Sibley and Jacob, such resistance can be "more constructive than much of the relatively useless work carried on in C. P. S. And the [subsequent] lives of many of the absolutists seemed to show that their dramatic acts of resistance during the war were not ends in themselves" (417).

Still, absolutism tended to exacerbate the already individualistic character of conscientious objection. In other words, the legal definition of conscientious objection had necessarily produced a population whose very resistance was often predicated upon individualized dissent rather than group dissent. But despite the individualistic character of these dissenters, resistance was not limited to individual acts alone. The proponents of active resistance saw it as "making pacifism and conscientious objection a truly political movement," while its detractors saw it as "violent and intolerant of others" (Sibley and Jacob 467). Moreover, "many members of the Historic Peace Churches . . . questioned the necessity and desirability of refusals to work and eat" because these refusals resembled the tactics of warfare (373). In spite of the debates within the conscientious objector community, active resistance, both individual and collective, manifested itself most dramatically in U.S. prisons during the war, where resisters tested the limits of state power and searched for ways to assert their freedom.

CONSCIENTIOUS OBJECTORS IN PRISON DURING WORLD WAR II

Of the fifty thousand American conscientious objectors during World War II, about six thousand objectors went to prison (Zahn v–vi). After 1942, 90 percent of war resisters served multiyear sentences (Sibley and Jacob 353). Though the number of C. O. prisoners was relatively small, they vastly outnumbered their World War I counterparts and constituted a significant portion of the prison population as a whole. The objectors from World War II were, according to Howard Zinn, "four times the number of C. O.'s who went to prison during World War I. Of every six men in federal prison, one was there as a C. O." (409). On the surface, the sheer number seems to offer an explanation for the resistance of objectors during the war. However, Jehovah's Witnesses comprised 75 percent of the objector prison population and, for the most part, did not share the social activist philosophy that drove the radical pacifist contributors to *Prison Etiquette* (Sibley and Jacob 355). The Jehovah's Witnesses' refusals to serve were based on theological grounds, not on radical or anarchist positions. In fact, "only 5.4 percent of all those sentenced were classified as philosophical or political objectors; all the rest . . . were presumably 'religious objectors'" (354).

The writers of *Prison Etiquette* comprised a small core of radicals, pacifists, and anarcho-pacifists, who, according to the Bureau of Prisons, were "'the most difficult group of conscientious objectors . . . reformer[s] with a zeal for changing the social, political, economic, and cultural order. Objection to war frequently is only one element in his program. He objects to many things, including the present military system'" (358). A. J. Muste, one of the leaders of the antiwar movement at the time, called for a pacifism that would be a movement for justice that would "make effective contacts with oppressed and minority groups such as Negroes, sharecroppers, [and] industrial workers" (Wittner 63). The C. O.'s in prison were up to the challenge.

Some resisters, like Lowell Naeve, escalated from acts of individual resistance to involvement in wider strikes; others, like Jim Peck, organized collective strikes to empower objectors to change prison conditions. Although both Naeve and Peck were radical pacifists, their experiences and their writings point to the broad range of differences among hardcore refusers. While Peck cut his political teeth in the labor movement, organizing sailors into democratic unions, Naeve developed his own personal anarchism, refusing to vote, even in a small group of striking C. O.'s. Ralph DiGia, another of the Danbury Prison strikers, recently recalled, "We would have votes, and [Naeve] wouldn't vote. We'd say, for God sakes, Lowell, it's just us, you know, we're a small group here, eighteen people and you won't vote? He said, I'm against voting. Okay, Lowell, don't vote" (DiGia).

The accounts by Jim Peck ("The Ship That Would Never Hit Port") and Lowell Naeve ("A Field of Broken Stones"), both participants in the Danbury Prison strike to desegregate the mess hall, demonstrate the range of personalities and ideological affiliations of the prison resisters. But because both of the accounts in *Prison Etiquette* are fragments of longer narratives, it is essential to refer to Peck's and Naeve's memoirs to tell the story of the Danbury Prison strike to desegregate the prison dining hall. The strike was one of the most important accomplishments of conscientious objectors during World War II and therefore deserves mention.

THE 1943 DANBURY PRISON STRIKE AGAINST SEGREGATION: NAEVE AND PECK

Both Lowell Naeve and Jim Peck began their memoirs of war resistance while in prison; each writer reflected on the origins of their resistance, their psychological experience in prison, and their involvement in prison activism. It should be noted, first and foremost, that the very existence of Naeve's memoir, *A Field of Broken Stones,* is a testament to the artist's ingenuity; with the help of fellow war resister David Wieck, Naeve smuggled out the only unconfiscated copy of the book in a hollow papier-mâché frame for one of his paintings. In his memoir, Naeve recalls that his pacifism emerged both from personal conviction—an early experience of killing a rabbit disgusted him—and from class awareness, that "war was to enrich munitions millionaires, to protect Standard Oil properties abroad, etc." (*A Field of Broken Stones* 6). Naeve's refusal was individual, unaffiliated with any religious or political organization.

Jim Peck, in contrast to Naeve, had long participated in radical politics; rebelling against his bourgeois family, Peck attended his first demonstration in New York in 1933, to protest the Nazi Party. After scandalizing his Harvard class by bringing a black woman to the freshman prom, he dropped out and joined the union struggle while working on freighters. His opposition to war led him to begin writing for the War Resisters League's newspaper, *The Conscientious Objector;* he refused to sign his draft card and was sentenced to three years in November 1942.

Naeve's memoir is hauntingly written; its spare prose and angular pencil drawings create a claustrophobic, Kafkaesque atmosphere that reflects the trauma of entering prison. Naeve's initial experience of shocked submission soon dissipated as he began to make small refusals; on his fifth day at Danbury, he stopped working. In a surprising gesture of goodwill, the warden offered Naeve a studio in which to paint. However, Naeve rapidly realized the warden was using him as an example of the humane conditions in the prison; when he grew tired of being interrupted by visits from the warden and prison tourists, he declined outsiders access to the studio. Later, when ordered to paint some signs for the war, Naeve refused absolutely. The prison guards had to carry Naeve back to his cell, where he remained until he served out the sentence. Eight months later, however, he was arrested again for not having a draft card. This time, he was sent to Bellevue for psychiatric testing after he protested in solidarity with two C. O. hunger strikers, Stanley Murphy and Louis Taylor, who believed all refusers should be set free. There, he was force fed and drugged, until people heard of his treatment and started writing to him and visiting him in prison.

In contrast to Naeve's haunting prose, Peck's writing is marked by a hipster machismo, full of prison lingo, that anticipates Holden Caulfield: "In jail I found that the inmates are no different from any group of men picked at random on the outside. There is the same percentage of regular guys, the same percentage of phonies" (*Prison Etiquette* 49). He told a visitor to the prison that "'behind this phoney façade is the most completely fascist setup you can imagine'"(62). Peck, along with Naeve and other prisoners, began striking, perhaps as a way to survive the psychological damage of imprisonment. Peck's experience in union organizing helped him galvanize the prisoners. Prisoners—both cons and war resisters—began with hunger strikes (a "potato boycott" and a "scrap the scrapple boycott") and later expanded to strike against weekend work (landing them one week in solitary). Later, the C. O.'s refused to paint victory signs (giving them ten days in solitary and twenty-eight months in segregation). In his memoir, Peck acknowledges that though one might think that C. O.'s might be united by common goals, "the individualistic CO's at Danbury found it almost impossible to agree on any common action to support their cause" (*Underdogs* 38). Although it was difficult to organize such independent thinkers, strikes by C. O.'s had begun years earlier, initiated by Dave Dellinger and the other Union Theological Seminary students in 1940, and later brought to a dramatic crescendo in the highly publicized eighty-four-day hunger strike by Stanley Murphy and Louis Taylor protesting the imprisonment of C. O.'s. After the moderate successes of earlier strikes, the Danbury C. O.'s, led by Peck, decided to turn their attention to the segregation of the dining hall in Danbury Prison. In 1943, no prison had yet been desegregated; the Danbury C. O. strike, therefore, anticipated and informed the civil rights movement of the 1950s.

On August 11, 1943, Peck and seventeen others began the strike to end dining hall segregation; because of the large number of strikers, the prison had to construct a number of new separate "segregation" cells away from the rest of the prisoners. The strikers, allowed less than an hour outside per day, first communicated by yelling under the doors and often traded newspapers and cigarettes through an ingenious system of string and radiator rings. Lowell Naeve began a newspaper called The Clink by washing the ink from a copy of *Life* magazine. Naeve also made a guitar out of papier-mâché. Peck even wrote a song that the strikers performed, which included the following lyrics:

> They say that Hitler is wicked
> To persecute race in his way
> But when it's done in the U.S.
> It's quite perfectly o.k.
>
> The blacks are as good as the whites
> Why shouldn't they have equal rights
> The warden says no
> But we tell him it's so
> Jim crow must go.
>
> <div align="right">(<i>Underdogs</i> 49)</div>

While Peck's account emphasizes the solidarity, humor, and creativity of the struggle in his account, Naeve's account underscores the difficulty of community, as personal differences often threatened to break apart the strike. As the months dragged on, the strikers almost quit numerous times, as prison authorities seemed unperturbed by their resistance. However, when one striker's fiancé, Ruth MacAdam, "went to Harlem and persuaded Representative Adam Clayton Powell to organize a special committee in support of the strike," pressure on the prison authorities began to mount (*A Field of Broken Stones* 51). Two points deserve mention here. First, just as the civil rights movement would benefit from the government's fear of international embarrassment over its treatment of African Americans and other minorities, so too did the prison strike to desegregate the Danbury Prison mess hall benefit from alliances with African Americans like Powell. Second, the often unrecorded support by women for the war resisters was absolutely essential to the success of the strike and to the larger efforts of war resistance. David Dellinger recalled how "[women] had a less spectacular, more difficult path to journey without being adequately recognized as the brave and often lonely pioneers of a better future" (Hurwitz and Simpson). Only recent accounts, such as Rachel Waltner Goossen's *Women Against the Good War: Conscientious Objection and Gender on the American Home Front, 1941–1947* (1997) and Susan Schweik's *A Gulf So Deeply Cut: American Women Poets and the Second World War* (1991), have begun to consider the crucial importance of women to war resistance.

Nearly five months later, the warden finally agreed to end segregation in the dining hall, and Danbury Prison became the first federal prison to abolish segregation. Peck called the strike "one of the most important accomplishments of CO's in world war 2" (*Underdogs* 53). Some of the strikers almost immediately began new strikes, particularly against the continued imprisonment of C. O.'s; some of the strikers, including Naeve, even went on hunger strikes. As resistance escalated, the prison authorities split up the most hardcore resisters to different prisons. Naeve and Peck both served many more years; Naeve later immigrated to Canada, while Peck continued to fight oppression in the United States.

At the end of *Underdogs Vs Upperdogs,* Peck proudly displays a list of subsequent arrests; from his early arrests for union organizing, to Vietnam-era protests in the late 1960s, Peck's dissent reads like a "greatest hits" of protest from 1940 to 1970. After World War II, Peck protested the Bikini bomb explosions in 1946 and publicly burned his draft card in 1947, some twenty years prior to similar protests during the Vietnam War. In 1955, he participated in one of the first protests of civil defense drills in New York City with the Catholic Worker; in 1958, he sailed the *Golden Rule* with Albert Bigelow into an atomic test zone outside Hawaii. Most importantly, Peck continued his work challenging racial segregation by participating in the 1947 Journey of Reconciliation (sponsored by the C. O.-led groups Fellowship of Reconciliation and Congress of Racial Equality), one year after the Irene

Morgan ruling banned segregation on interstate buses; two World War II C. O.'s, George Houser and Bayard Rustin, organized the event. Later, in 1961, Peck joined the Freedom Rides (the only direct link to the earlier Journey of Reconciliation) to challenge the federal government to uphold the Bruce Boynton case, which called for the desegregation of all facilities used by interstate travelers. The Freedom Rides, traveling through the Deep South, encountered violent resistance. On May 14, near Anniston, Alabama, a Freedom Riders' bus was attacked and then bombed by an angry white mob. Peck was nearly beaten to death in Birmingham. Still, the white violence and the courage of the Riders brought national attention to the ongoing struggle against racism and helped end the segregation of all interstate travel.

FRAMING *PRISON ETIQUETTE*

When editors Holley Cantine and Dachine Rainer first published *Prison Etiquette* in 1950, as a "compendium of useful information," as its subtitle goes, they wanted to guard against the "commemorative" impulse that so often domesticates dissent or resistance movements. Still, it is the dynamic tension between utility and memory, between past and future, which propels the writings in *Prison Etiquette.* There is a utility in a movement remembering itself. For example, Howard Schoenfeld's "The Danbury Story," protesting the warden's withdrawal of permission to hold a demonstration, provides enough mundane details about prison life to demystify the prison institution, even as it documents an early C. O. victory in 1941. Schoenfeld recounts how the importance of a pitcher named Benedict to the Danbury softball team led the warden finally to agree to the C. O.s' demands and how their release led to "a mass catharsis [for all the prisoners]. . . . Some of the men were weeping, others were laughing like madmen. It was like nothing I had ever seen before, and nothing I ever expect to see again" (26).

By contrast, the elision of the successful conclusion to the 1943 desegregation strike, in both the Peck and Naeve selections, demonstrates that Cantine and Rainer believed that providing information about prison life and the possibilities of prison resistance was more important than documenting the specific triumphs of an individual strike. The editors' emphasis, even in the more descriptive second section of the anthology, works against the tendency to romanticize the resisters and to dissociate C. O. prison life from the life of the other inmates. Both Curtis Zahn, in "Notes on My Life Among the Dead Men in Denims," and Don Devault, in "McNeil Island," draw detailed portraits of their fellow prison inmates—a Blackfoot Indian, an Eskimo—who comprise the "island" of the prison community. In "Notes on the Prison Community," Bernard Phillips analyzes the functions of the prison system, its systems of control, its general structure, and its psychological pressures on the prisoners.

The final section, largely devoted to the creative expressions of war resisters, recounts the failures and successes of C. O. attempts to stage theater for fellow inmates, including a truncated version of the opera *Pagliacci* (Franklyn's "The Prison Theatre"). The tone and structure of poems by Arthur Kassin, James Holmes, E. R. Karr, and Lowell Naeve range from the humorously ironic to the existential, from free verse to sonnet. Although these creative endeavors are worthy of mention, a more complete account of C. O. literature has yet to be written. At the very least, the account would include William Stafford's memoir *Down in My Heart* and poems by Robert Lowell and William Everson. However, it is Naeve's pencil drawing, appearing throughout *Prison Etiquette,* that is perhaps the most fascinating and haunting creative expression of the prison experience. The drawings delineate the existential loneliness of prison, the way in which it infiltrates the minds of inmates and guards alike. Frequently superimposing human figures against prison architecture, Naeve invokes the internalization of punishment and the diminishment of the individual.

The final two letters offer a sobering critique of the prison system and a call to resistance. William H. Kuenning's "Letter to a Penologist" replies to a questionnaire by questioning its very presumptions and calls for the abolition of the prison system. Jack Hewelike's "Letter" credits the small, less public and less organized acts of resistance by all prisoners "directed against imprisonment itself" (137). For Hewelike, the publicity given to cases of physical brutality overshadows "the less sensational but far more important role of this prison—beating down all resistance and crushing all individuality" (138).

LEGACIES OF RADICAL PACIFISM DURING WORLD WAR II

The experience of war resistance often had a paradoxical effect. On the one hand, objectors were alienated from mainstream society, geographically and psychologically marginalized, an exilic condition that forced each objector to "serve his own time," as the saying went. On the other hand, objection brought together a diverse group, from religious pacifists to secular anarchists, and led to crucial conversations about the meaning and possibilities of resistance.

Whether the experience of conscientious objection encouraged writing as a mode of resistance or whether writers themselves were more likely to refuse to bear arms is difficult to say. However, the fact that several major poets and writers emerged from internment totally refutes the notion that politics and literary arts are incompatible—Robert Lowell, William Stafford, William Everson, and J. F. Powers all have made important contributions to American literature. Lowell is arguably the most important postwar American poet, and Everson was a pivotal figure in the San Francisco Renaissance and Beat Poetry movements. Other major pacifist poets include Stanley Kunitz, who refused to bear arms and was forced to go through basic training three times; Kenneth Rexroth, who worked in a mental hospital; and Robert Duncan and avant-garde poet Jackson Mac Low, who both received IV-F waivers.

War resistance during World War II, therefore, has two intertwined legacies: one of literary innovation and one of political activism. In *An Energy Field More Intense Than War: The Nonviolent Tradition and American Literature,* Michael True asserts that World War II, paradoxically, was "one of the richest periods for the nonviolent tradition in literature" (75), of which *Prison Etiquette* is an essential part. The Civilian Public Service camps and the prisons where C. O.'s served became sites of creative and political resistance, from which numerous poets, writers, and activists worked out the sentences of their beliefs. These experimenters in artistic and social action would later become crucial participants in the civil rights and peace movements of the late 1950s and 1960s. David Dellinger, one of the Union Theological Seminary objectors, would later become a leader in the peace movement during the Vietnam War; James Farmer, George Houser, Jim Peck, and Bayard Rustin would propel the civil rights movement.

Houser, for example, helped form the Congress of Racial Equality with James Farmer in 1942 and actively confronted *de facto* segregation at Chicago's White City Roller Rink (April 1942), the University of Chicago's barber shop, and various restaurants, most memorably at Stoner's in the Loop (1943, see Tracy 32–33). Houser also helped plan the Journey of Reconciliation, the aforementioned precursor to the Freedom Rides in 1961; seven of the sixteen participants were C. O.'s, two black and five white. Rustin would later organize the 1963 March on Washington and was an essential figure in Martin Luther King's inner circle, providing a "wealth of tactical experience . . . informing King's conclusion that there was a viable nonviolent path to a successful outcome in the boycott" (Tracy 96). Two other C. O.'s, Lew Hill and Roy Kepler, would found Pacifica Radio at KPFA in the Bay Area. Finally, Gordon Zahn, Larry Gara, and others would become influential academics.

In *Direct Action: Radical Pacifism from the Union Eight to the Chicago Seven,* James Tracy emphasizes the radical pacifists' indelible contribution to American dissent during the Cold War, particularly through their founding involvement in groups like the Congress of Racial Equality, the War Resisters League, the Fellowship of Reconciliation, and the Committee for Nonviolent Action. For Tracy, their reliance was on

> tactical commitment to direct action; an agenda that posited race and militarism (instead of labor) as the central social issues of the United States; an experimental protest style that emphasized media-savvy, symbolic confrontation with institutions deemed oppressive; an ethos that privileged action over analysis and extolled nonviolent individual resistance, especially when it involved 'putting one's body on the line'; and an organized structure that was nonhierarchical, decentralized, and oriented toward consensus making. Genealogies of the Civil Rights, antiwar, and antinuclear movements in this period are incomplete without understanding the history of radical pacifism. (xiv)

At the same time, Tracy argues that radical pacifists leave an "ambivalent legacy" (153); while they created singular acts of dissent during the most oppressive periods of the Cold War in the 1940s and 1950s, they also contributed to "the ultimate unraveling of the Left in the late 1960s" (xv). Perhaps Tracy places the blame unfairly on the shoulders of the radical pacifists, given the confluence of mitigating factors that conspired to derail progressivism in the United States—the collusion of labor unions with management, the Vietnam War, the fragmentation of the antiwar movement after 1968, the reactionary turn of the Silent Majority and the rise of neoconservatism. Rather, the radical pacifist emphasis on actions designed for media attention, often sustained by a kind of macho individualist resistance, found its historical limit on the streets of Berkeley and Chicago.

Tracy notes that "for those who forged the radical pacifist movement, the inviolable constitutive unit of society was the individual . . . theirs was a thoroughly American radicalism" (40). The radical pacifists rejected Soviet communism as vociferously as American capitalism, and their distrust of authority—which they saw in the U.S. as leading toward totalitarianism—led them to "a rather mystical commitment to total Democracy" (40) and an orientation that A. J. Muste termed "holy disobedience." Certainly, the writings of *Prison Etiquette* bear out Tracy's thesis that radical pacifists perceived themselves as individuals locked in a war against a system that crushes conformity. In this way, then, the radical pacifists embody a Thoreauvian individualism; they did not scorn all social organization, only the state and, in particular, the cultural formation about which even Eisenhower would warn the American public—the military-industrial complex. If, at times, the radical pacifists sound shrill in their protest, it is important to remember the conditions under which they composed these lines.

Amid the flood of prose writers fawning over the "greatest" generation and World War II, the republication of *Prison Etiquette* could not be timelier, casting a cold Foucauldian eye at what war resisters saw as a society that increasingly resembled a prison. In light of the social repression of the containment 1950s, *Prison Etiquette* is prophetic. Even if its anarchist compilers intended their anthology to be a guide for surviving prison, it now reads as an inspiring, and often harrowing, account of resistance. Along with *A Few Small Candles: War Resisters from World War II Tell Their Stories* (1999) and *Women Against the Good War* (1997), *Prison Etiquette*'s republication signifies a renewed excavation of the half-buried history of American dissenters during World War II.

Finally, it is important to note that *Prison Etiquette* takes its place among the literatures both of war resistance and of prison resistance. Since the 1980s and the "war on drugs," the prison industry has expanded at a record pace. Today, the "prison-industrial complex" now houses two million inmates; as an increasingly privatized industry, it appears to be ensuring that it will continue to *produce* the product (criminals) necessary to expand to its full market potential. And yet, prison resistance continues unabated, in many forms, as assertions of individual and collective protest against a system that continues to administer punishments overwhelmingly against the poor and racial minorities. According to Bell Gale Chevigny, "the writing coming out of U.S. prisons has never been as strong, rich, diverse, and provocative as in the final quarter of the twentieth century" (xiii).

The prison actions of war resisters during World War II, in other words, were more than symbolic actions of protest; they were the first assertions that would later flower into the creative and political movements of the late 1950s and 1960s and into our present day. In the words of fellow conscientious objector William Stafford,

> our chance to live depends on such a sign
> while others talk and the Pentagon from the moon
> is bouncing exact commands: "Forget your faith;
> be ready for whatever it takes to win: we face
> annihilation unless all citizens get in line."

(181)

SELECTED BIBLIOGRAPHY

Chevigny, Bell Gale, ed. *Doing Time: 25 Years of Prison Writing.* New York: Arcade Publishing, 1999.

Cooney, Robert, and Helen Michalowski, eds. *The Power of the People: Active Nonviolence in the United States.* Culver City, CA: Peace Press, 1977.

DiGia, Ralph. Interview by Philip Metres. October 1999.

Gara, Larry and Lenna Mae. *A Few Small Candles: War Resisters of World War II Tell Their Stories.* Kent: Kent State UP, 1999.

Hamilton, Ian. *Robert Lowell: A Biography.* NY: Random House, 1982.

Hurwitz, Deena, and Craig Simpson, eds. *Against the Tide: Pacifist Resistance in the Second World War, an Oral History.* New York: War Resisters League, 1984. N. pag.

Lowell, Robert. *Selected Poems.* New York: Farrar Straus and Giroux, 1976.

Musto, Ronald G. *The Catholic Peace Tradition.* Maryknoll, NY: Orbis, 1986.

Naeve, Lowell. *A Field of Broken Stones.* Glen Gardner, NJ: Libertarian Press, 1950.

Peck, James. *Underdogs Vs Upperdogs.* Canterbury, NH: Greenleaf Books, 1969.

Sibley, Mulford Q., and Philip E. Jacob. *Conscription of Conscience: The American State and the Conscientious Objector, 1940–1947.* Ithaca: Cornell UP, 1952.

Stafford, William. *The Way It is: New and Selected Poems.* St. Paul: Graywolf, 1998.

Tracy, James. *Direct Action: From the Union Eight to the Chicago Seven.* Chicago: U of Chicago P, 1996.

True, Michael. *An Energy Field More Intense Than War: The Nonviolent Tradition and American Literature.* Syracuse: Syracuse UP, 1995.

Wittner, Lawrence. *Rebels Against War: The American Peace Movement 1933–1983.* Philadelphia: Temple UP, 1984.

Zahn, Gordon. *Another Part of the War: The Camp Simon Story.* Amherst: U of Massachusetts P, 1979.

Zinn, Howard. *A People's History of the United States.* New York: HarperPerennial, 1990.

PREFACE

CHRISTOPHER ISHERWOOD

The men who have written this book were all members of the extreme pacifist minority which resisted the U.S. conscription system during World War II. *Extreme pacifist* is the best description I can think of, but it is unsatisfactory and vague; for the group contained several sorts of anarchists, individualists, religious and non-religious objectors. Some of them had refused even to register for the draft, holding that registration itself implies acceptance of the military machine; others, having registered, found themselves unable to accept any of the compromises offered to the conscientious objectors by the State—forestry camps, medical projects, or non-combatant service with the armed forces. So they chose prison, and served terms ranging from one to five years in various penitentiaries and road camps, up and down the country. Some were even arrested and sentenced twice.

PRISON ETIQUETTE may, as its title indicates, be regarded simply as a manual of living-technique for prisoners in general. It is also a statement, written with great power, insight and occasional humor, of the whole anarchist-pacifist position. As such, it will have its own, necessarily limited appeal. But I want to recommend it, now, to a far wider public.

Maybe you will never go to prison, either willingly or unwillingly. Maybe you disagree completely with the stand which these men took, or feel, at any rate that they were unreasonably radical and unnecessarily uncooperative. (I myself was a law-abiding and somewhat apologetic objector during the same period.) But that is neither here nor there. For the problems raised by this book extend far beyond the usual catagories of 'right' and 'wrong', expediency and inexpediency. They touch all our lives.

We all—much as we may hate to admit it—have a foot in both camps. Each one of us is an individual. Each one of us has a measure of responsibility for the existing machinery of the law-making and law-enforcing State. We may imagine that the relation between our individual and our social selves is stabilized, permanently adjusted. It is not. It cannot be. It ought not to be.

Therefore we all owe an enormous debt of gratitude to those daring and dissatisfied spirits who strike out, no matter why, into the dangerous no-man's-land beyond the laws and the social conventions, to find the inner truth of our human relationships and to restate it in action. By a sort of atomic fission, they generate new and terrific discharges of power from old, worn-out, everyday words like 'brotherhood', 'peace', 'compassion'. Such men have much in common with those few genuinely original artists who, in every age, restate the inner truth of form, sound, color, and meaning. The artist challenges and forces us to re-examine our ingrown habits of perceiving and feeling. The anarchist-objector forces us to re-examine our habits of social thinking and the society which represents them.

All of these men have suffered, physically and psychologically, in a way which most of us can hardly even imagine. Yet it would be as absurd and insulting to offer them our pity as to feel sorry for Baudelaire or Van Gogh. Our tribute to their endurance must be this: that we try with all our might to understand what their action meant to them, what it means to ourselves, and why it was necessary. If we honestly do that, then we can say, not callously, but with grateful humility that their sufferings were well worth while.

I hope (and I am sure the authors hope) that this book will not be dismissed, or too easily accepted, as just another indictment of the U.S. prison system. It is so very much more than that. And indeed, the wardens and guards who appear, very fairly presented, in these pages, are more often bewildered and half-apologetically reproachful than positively brutal. ("You fellows do so much objecting that if we opened the gate right now and told you to go home, some of you would get half way out and then come back and object about that.") One can sympathize with them even at their worst. A lifetime of routine and rule-of-thumb psychology in dealing with ordinary prisoners is unlikely to prepare you for a man like Lowell Naeve. The average type of guard could not possibly be subjected to a more exquisite form of mental torture than passive resistance. No wonder if some of them cracked under the strain and responded with acts of violence.

Certainly, there are prisons in this country which are very bad, and no doubt much could be done to reform them, even within the framework of the existing penal system. It goes without saying that such reforms are desirable; but, in working for them, we must never allow ourselves to forget that the great central problem remains unsolved—the problem of Man's freedom within Society. Because this book sets that problem squarely before you, I wish it could be read by everybody in the United States.

ACKNOWLEDGMENTS

We wish to thank the fifteen contributors for their material and for accepting our editing, Christopher Isherwood for the preface, Lowell Naeve for the eleven illustrations, and Kaj Klitgaard for the original jacket design.

To James Laughlin who donated the half ton of paper for PRISON ETIQUETTE, Sandor Katz who donated the coverboard, Margaret De Silver and the other individuals who contributed their enthusiasm, time, and money during the two years we were editing and printing this book, our boundless gratitude.

The final thanks of all of us are due the readers for their support, which will enable us to go on to new and better infamies.

Holley Cantine
Dachine Rainer

INTRODUCTION

PRISON ETIQUETTE is "the convicts' compendium of useful information". We are publishing it neither because we want to reform the Prison System, nor merely to honor the valor and integrity of its contributors who, because of their convictions, spent up to three years in the Federal Penitentiaries of this country.

We *are* publishing PRISON ETIQUETTE in order to present the experiences of some of the several thousand Conscientious Objectors to World War II. Many of them salvaged from their years of captivity ideas of immeasurable value to all of us who contemplate in the coming totalitarian days a continual warfare with the state—both in and out of its prisons.

Prison etiquette is a learned art for the radical. Its technique varies with country, time, and political set-up. These young men deal with a prison system that is unknown to us. We must be equipped to evade it, to survive in it if caught, to resist it in the psychologically most economical, and politically effective way. That is, we must learn to remain sane, to survive physically, and at the same to continue resisting.

This book is not a commemorative exercise. It is a practical book that we have edited in a manner calculated to provide our reader with what may unfortunately become useful information.

II

There is one loss sustained in prison that transcends in poignancy the numerous comparatively trivial pains and material discomforts—: it is the idea of being unfree. Imprisonment is a violation of the fundamental nature of human existence which is predicated on a certain amount of freedom of choice and movement. While obviously no such thing as total freedom can exist owing to the biological and intellectual limitations of man, man exists in the Prison in an almost total absense of free motion and choice.

These two qualities are meaningful only if both are present simultaneously. That is, if one can proceed from the idea to the act, or from the choice to the fulfillment. This is almost never the case in Prison. The arbitrary separation and curtailment of these two freedoms that define the individual is the essence of Imprisonment—; the entire system is predicated on the conscious and systematic destruction of the Person. When the Prisoner is not under direct surveillance he is confined in a narrow space, and when he is allowed some freedom of motion, he is subjected to the strictest kind of regimentation.

When he is locked into his cell, where he is allowed freedom to think, no acts may follow from that thinking that can affect either his Prison environment or the other prisoners—unless the disobeys Prison rules in some manner. When he moves about outside his cell, it is under orders—in lines or in work detachments. This abrogation of the essence of the individual destroys not only each single person, but consequently, any possibility of community —except again, when Prison rules are disobeyed. For while the prisoner is free to think, or perform a limited number of acts involving his own person—even suicide is made very difficult—he is allowed little, if any, interpersonal relationships. The individual prisoner lives either in a dormitory, where he has no privacy, or he lives in relative or absolute isolation, where he has little or no opportunity to communicate with anyone; these two situations can exist alternately for the same individual.

The effect of all this is to produce an intense egocentricity that is almost infantile. It is calculated to create a docile easily controlled Prison population, that is largely incapable of organizing resistance.

III

Prison is the only key political institution that is peculiar to the State form of society. Armies, courts, schools, legislative bodies exist, at least in embryo, in nearly all other social forms. But the Prison exists only in highly centralized systems. It is the most perfect expression of the full implications of Statism. In the Prison the population is subjected to the type of control that State functionaries aspire to impose on the population "at large". The Prison represents absolute freedom of coercion.

The stronger the State becomes the more laws it passes and the more the area of potential lawbreaking is increased. Old-fashioned notions of guilt and innocence, crime and respectable behavior, become meaningless in the tangled web of the laws and regulations of a totalitarian State. Everybody is guilty of innumerable offenses and escapes incarceration only through chance. While the United States has yet to achieve this degree of uniformity in the culpability of its population, it is moving in that direction, and many individuals who have little in common with the old concept of the professional criminal may find themselves in trouble with the authorities.

The old-fashioned radical, not unlike the professional criminal, lived in continual expectation of going to prison; if he had not done time on various occasions himself, he was sure to have acquaintances who had, and the experience, when it came, as it was almost certain to, was therefore neither unexpected nor entirely unprepared for, emotionally as well as intellectually. For the past few decades, however, except for those war resisters who spent time in Prison for refusing military service, the number who have been arrested, let alone imprisoned, has been comparitively small in this country. The reasons for this need not be gone into here, but it obvious that this situation is changing rapidly and the luck of the radical seems about to take a sharp turn for the worse. Therefore, in order to fill, at least partially, the gap in experience and psychological preparation that was created during the New Deal honeymoon between radicalism and the government we feel that some current information on Prison conditions should be of considerable service to those who now face imprisonment for their ideas. The old-timers in the movement, while they unquestionaby know a great deal about Prison conditions of twenty or more years ago, are probably not so familiar with the current situation, and the younger generation, for the most part, has neither first nor second-hand knowledge of it.

IV

One thing we are *not* trying to accomplish is Prison reform. The existing Prison system in the United States is, in many ways, the most thoroughly reformed in the world as it is, but we have never heard of anyone whose stay in it was greatly alleviated on this account.✦

Reforming an institution like Prison is only possible on the most superficial level, and its importance to the individual prisoner is highly questionable. The fact of incarceration is the one thing that can never be removed by reform; that is, the fact that one is confined to a place in which he would much rather not be, and beside this such considerations as food, cleanliness, recreation, etc. —provided they do not sink to the level where survival itself is endangered—are of distinctly secondary importance.

It may even be harder, for psychological reason, to endure the new sort of "honor system" Prison, in which the prisoner is made to feel personally responsible for his own captivity, than the old, frankly autocratic and brutally coercive type of institution. Giving the inmates a greater say about how their lives are to be run in Prison is at best hypocrisy, inasmuch as none of them would be

---

✦ The improvement in the material conditions in American Prisons in the interval between the First and Second World Wars is considerable. The food is better, there are better accomodations, more light, air, exercise; the beatings, deprivations, solitary are less frequent, and plumbing is conspicuously present. We do not believe that these gains have occurred through liberal intervention, but probably through such fortuitous factors as the Prohibition Era, which resulted in the imprisonment of high-grade 'criminals' who could bribe for improvements, and perhaps the graft involved in letting plumbing contracts for Prison installations.

there at all if they could help it; and at worst, the sort of horror that existed in the Nazi concentration camps, where nearly all custodial functions were performed by inmates (under supervision of course) with consequences, in terms of brutalization and degradation, that surpass anything in the history of the Prison.

Agitation for Prison reform is a thoroughly futile activity since Prisons never *stay* reformed. Russian and German Prisons under the relative utopias of the Czar and Kaiser, respectively, provided—at least for their political prisoners—a reasonably comfortable existence, in which it was possible to devote considerable time to study. At this time—that is, prior to and during World War I—conditions for political prisoners in American Prisons were worse than for criminals and among the worst in the world. Living conditions were intolerable, and beatings were common. In the space of a generation the situations have been reversed; conditions in American Prisons have been greatly ameliorated[*]; and everyone knows about the Nazi German and Soviet Russian concentration camps.

V

The contributors to this volume were political prisoners but our opposition to imprisonment extends not merely to *their* imprisonment, but to the whole concept of the Prison. Imprisonment is gratuitous punishment: except for the liberal penologist—there is no one, neither Prisoner nor guard, who would testify to its rehabilitating effects. Prison fails to discourage "crime"; it insures its increase. Moreover, a great deal of what is considered punishable as "crime" does not deserve to be punished or even discouraged. Obviously it is a clear violation of the most elementary concept of civil liberties to punish people for holding an opinion, no matter how contrary it is to the generally accepted one. But apart from this, and apart from the fact that many individuals are

---

[*] Except in Springfield, Mo., the Federal Prison system's 'mental hospital', where the old order still remains--numerous beatings and psychological terror. Prisoners who are 'difficult'--that is, any prisoner who refuses to submit to the 'normal' Prison regime is 'bugged' and sent to Springfield. The threat of being sent there is continually held over the heads of all Federal Inmates.

arrested for offenses they never committed—but in order that some cop meet his quota of arrests, and are convicted in order that some Prosecuting Attorney meet his quota of convictions—how much of what is generally considered to be crime is so because of arbitrary definition?

One might agree that it is wrong to imprison people for their ideas, and certainly wrong to imprison them in frame-ups, but might feel the need to put away the "aggressors against society." What constitutes an aggression against society? Is it theft, murder assault, rape, arson? But is there ever any more arson committed than in the bombing of a city; is there ever any more assault and murder committed than in the course of a war? Is there ever any more rape and looting than by occupying troops? Yet the perpetrators of these crimes are held to be guiltless or even heroic and the initiator of the crime of warfare is that same institution, the State, which passes judgment on the relatively piddling crimes of individuals.

The numerous other crimes like counterfeiting and income tax evasion, are punished by the State because they undermine its power. But who, conceding that the State is the Arch Criminal, would wish to conserve or increase its power? It might more logically be argued that failure to pay one's income tax, considering the criminal purpose to which it is put, is an obligatory and virtuous act.

We do not wish to imply that the cases of individual social aggression, like arson, theft, etc., do not constitute something of a problem, but it is patently absurd to hold that the Great Thief, the Great Arsonist is at all equipped to pass judgment on the lesser ones✢.

✢ The whole concept of guilt and innocence, judgment and punishment is involved here. Judgment (except when it is private AND powerless) coexists with authority, and is an unmitigated evil. Any body of men, by virtue of their numbers and organization towards a common end is able to coerce the single man. It is by this democratic fallacy---which insists that numbers equal RIGHT, when numbers merely signify POWER, that the family may have evolved into the group, the group into the state, each with its inviolable right to judge and to coerce.

It seems that man in the group, even the very small group, perhaps even the family, is more than, and different from the sum total of the individual members of the unit I do not believe that the status of the individuals involved is significant --MERELY THE FACT OF COLLECTIVITY. Groups persecute individuals. For the

VI

We realize that a book of this sort should be primarily concerned with techniques for escaping, but unfortunately, such techniques are not easy to come by, for obvious reasons. We have had to content ourselves with the poor second best of relating methods by which one's stay in Prison can be alleviated as much as possible, giving as wide a choice of alternative methods as we could obtain. Different personalities will, of course, find different ways of enduring Prison. Pure individualists may find helpful suggestions in Lowell Naeve's example of absolute non-cooperation; more gregarious types, in the various pieces dealing with strikes and group resistance; and all should benefit from the practical ideas for achieving oblivion.

The importance of striking in Prison, whatever its particular objective, lies not so much in the end to be attained, as in the act itself. It is one way, and in some cases the only one, in which the individual can assert himself *as* an individual (or at least as a member of a group of his own choosing), rather than remain a mere object, to which the whole weight of institutional pressures, both conscious and unconscious, attempt to reduce him.

This, in our opinion, is the most important aspect of enduring Prison: to maintain as much as possible one's sense of being an individual. In some cases, it might even be true that winning a strike—for instance, one for greater democracy in running the Prison—would be worse, from a psychological standpoint, than losing it. For, to the degree one is made to feel responsible for his life in Prison (which is not at all the same as being responsible for his life) he ceases to be an an individual and thus ceases to possess those qualities which make survival itself meaningful.

HOLLEY CANTINE and DACHINE RAINER

the survival of the group--the survival of an organization, that is--no matter how loose, how circumscribed in function and power, it is essential that each individual give up a certain degree of individuality--contribute it, so to speak, to the group. The group therefore becomes something out of nothing and each individual that is part of it becomes something less than he was. In extreme cases, like the Prison, the organization is everything; the prisoner AND the guard nothing.   D.R.

PRISON ETIQUETTE

SECTION ONE

RESISTANCE IN PRISON

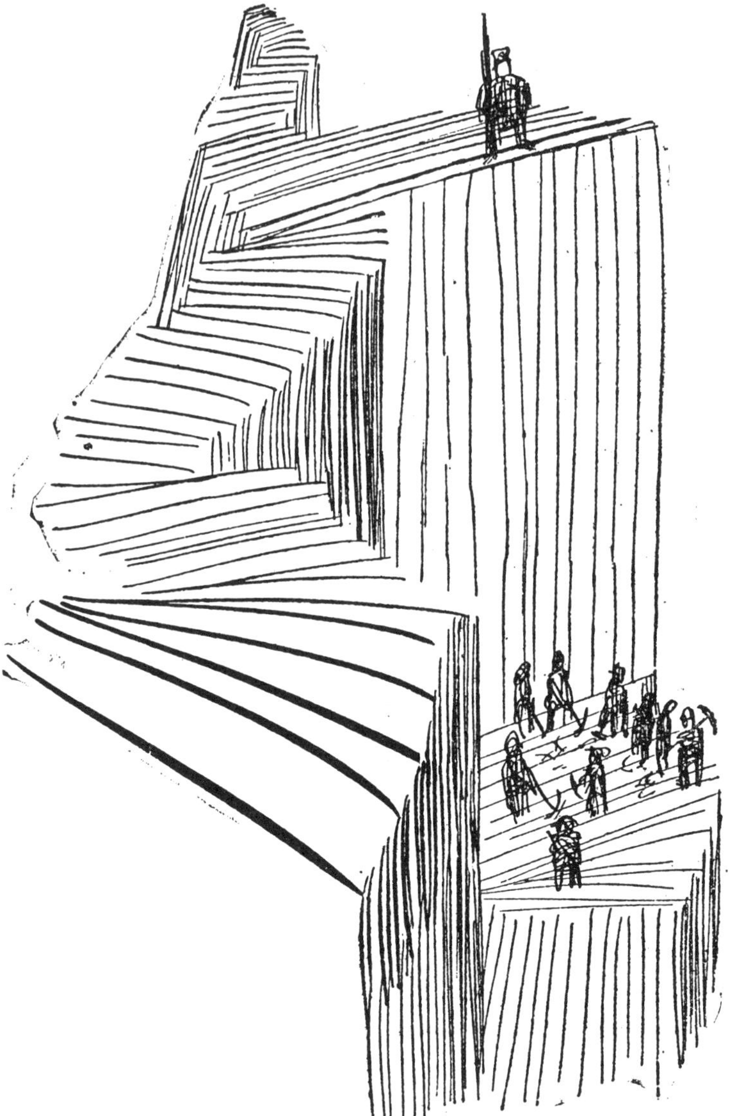

RESISTANCE IN PRISON

CLIF BENNETT

For those who want a preview of the American police state in action, complete with distinguishing variations from the European model, thirty-two Federal correctional and penal institutions offer unlimited research facilities. Entrance requirements are stiff, but the experience may prove invaluable to anyone looking for a slingshot to use against the new Goliath.

Organizing resistance within a prison requires an understanding of the inmate's state of mind. He cannot exercise initiative of choice, nor may he express himself freely in any way. His individuality is limited to making "Big Deal" talk with other cons about how many Packards and Billy Rose blondes wait for him outside the walls. With his ego thoroughly squashed and trampled on, he is further cramped emotionally by the prohibition against showing sympathy or solidarity with a mistreated fellow inmate. "Every man does his own time," is the iron sophistry of the walled city. The uniforms are there to see that you keep your eyes straight ahead while the man next to you is slugged and dragged down the corridor to the strip cell.

Thus starved for an opportunity to affirm their humanity, prisoners fall back heavily on the old American substitutes for honest emotion: Patriotism and Mama. The Federal prisons had one of the highest records in the country for War Bond sales. No cell is complete without a picture of Mama, and no issue of the prison paper escapes some maudlin Edgar Guest intent on explaining the particular virtues of his maternal parent.

The springboard for action which will restore some semblance of Man to the numbered fragments inside the wall is always some immediate grievance felt by the prison body as a whole or by some sizable group within it. Usually it is the prison food, which appears on the menu board in the mess hall under a variety of alluring names—and always turns out to be lumpy bread pudding.

Food strikes may be directed against the entire meal, with the men refusing to leave their quarters where possible, or marching through the mess hall with empty trays if attendance there is compelled. Where the action is directed against a specific item of food, inmates are wised up by the grapevine ahead of chow time and take everything but the objectionable food. As a variation of the food boycott directed against one item, the scrapple, rotten frankfurters or greasy potatoes may be taken, hidden in a scrap of paper, or paper napkin, and dropped to the walk upon leaving the mess hall. It is unlikely to reappear on the tables, particularly after the Associate Warden had to wade through it to Officers' Mess.

Since refusal to eat cannot usually be ferreted out as an assault on the prison administration, it is a good initial move prior to a strike. In both the minimum and maximum custody institutions, we found that a food boycott, once popular, tended naturally to become a work strike. Once the prisoners had refused a meal, they gathered in little groups in the yard. "No eat, no work," they said. And the hardier souls among them would refuse to report to their work detail.

The extreme form of the food boycott is the hunger strike. When a large number of men take this action, it cannot be expected to last more than a day or two at the longest. The hunger strike is better adapted to the use of individuals or small, highly dedicated groups with a long-range view of what is to be accomplished.

In any action taken by the prison population as a group, the initiators must be familiar with the routine steps to put down resistance, and the working rules for relations with the prison authorities during times of unrest. The prison officials will use:

(1) Soft soap. The confidence man on the prison staff, usually the Warden or an Associate Warden, will try to have the strikers herded into the auditorium and, with the prescribed combination of sternness and paternal concern, will promise them the moon if they get back into harness.

(2) Intimidation. This may be directed against the group as a whole, or individuals suspected as troublemakers may be weeded out and brought to the Warden's Office for a reprimand and warning. Solitary confinement, loss of 'good time', and shipment to a tougher pen are the usual threats.

[3] Violence. Pick handles are a favorite weapon. Water hoses are sometimes used; if one of these is brought into a cell block prison etiquette demands that you use mattresses and blankets for shelter so the officers may destroy prison property without your wasting energy on the job. Tear gas and guns are brought out only in extreme situations; the American prison guard does not as a rule develop a great deal of personal animosity even in critical moments. His attitude is "That's the regulations." He would undoubtedly lock up his own father with the same impersonal loyalty to the Officers' Manual.

To meet the inevitable soft soap, the strikers must have a clear idea of their objective. They must have a definite demand, or set of demands, which it is possible for the administration to meet They must agree before striking that they will not return to work until these demands are granted or the strike is broken by force. they must present these demands at the first chance.

To insure the continuation of the strike after the spokesmen are sent to solitary or shipped (usually in the middle of the night, or while the population is locked in cell blocks) a succession of leadership should be agreed on, with alternate contacts in each cell block.

When violence is used by the officials, passive resistance is most effective in prison. It is sometimes difficult to adhere to, but will result in increased sympathy from those not striking and will conserve the rebellious spirit of the men for future action. An excess of violence on the part of the the inmates, even in self-defense, will exhaust their ardor and postpone a resurgence for a long time. As in guerilla warfare, the objective is not the individual enemy, but his materials, means of communication and morale.

Leadership must be alert to all local developments of value to the strikers. In the Danbury prison strike of 1946 the administration was aware of plans for a strike because of news releases sent out by coordinating groups in the 'free world'. A fake demonstration was held in the prison yard on the day before the strike was scheduled in the hope that prison officials might think that was the limit of the disturbance. The following day was Lincoln's Birthday and the strike might have been a dismal failure had not the officials obligingly ordered all men to report to their work assigments on the morning of that day.

Danbury prison at that time held a large number of Negro Selective Service cases, most of whom worked in the prison industry, a glove factory. The initial agitation was therefore directed at the Negro cell block, with the result that the prison industry was closed down, half the population demonstrated and sang songs in the yard, and two or three hundred refused to be enticed into the mess hall by a chicken dinner.

At the same prison, the inmate paper was edited by a company man who diffused more than the ordinary smell of polecat. When he put out an issue urging acceptance of the officials' plan for an Inmate Advisory Council (company union), all available copies were gathered up in every cell block, tied together in a bundle and delivered to the Warden without comment.

In the Lewisburg strike of 1947, the administration put forward this company union proposal right in the middle of the fireworks. Slips of paper were distributed to every cell, so the inmate might indicate his choice of representatives for the projected pint-sized parliament. The sewage disposal system was jammed with paper slips for several hours.

Whether the political prisoners are segregated or mixed with the prison population, a few points of agreement will simplify the job. First, they should make no contract of any kind with the administration. Second, they should refuse to deal singly with any prison official on any matter that might conceivably be a group concern. Third, they should refrain from violence in defending themselves against officers.

Of course, the resister will find that a contract is 'assumed' between himself and the officials, and that certain things are 'expected' of him. There is, however, no pretense that the inmate has the right to change, or even to interpet, this assumed contract. Interpretations—several different ones to fit each situation—will come from the Warden's office.

In instances where the resisters are segregated in one cell block, and none of them has any illusions about making parole, a number of joyful pastimes are offered which are guaranteed to furnish gray hair for the Warden and a rapid transfer to maximum custody for those involved. If the cell doors are of the individual lock type plus a master control operated manually or electrically from a box available only to the officer, the entire cell block may bo put out of operation in a few minutes by stuffing paper clips, spring steel, fork tines and similar obstacles into the keyhole. In many prisons, the door hinges may be sprung by rolling a blanket tightly and inserting it on the hinge side while the door is swung closed against it. If the controls are operated entirely from a master box, and the doors are of the sliding variety, the keyhole on the master box may be be plugged if it can be reached.

Most prisons have a vulnerable ventilating system which opens into corridors through panels equipped with Allen head screws. An Allen head screwdriver may, with patience, be shaped from a large nail. The water supply and waste pipes are usually run in these ducts. This ventilating system is a hollow steel drum, and a proper beating administered in the panels by five or six men will carry through the entire institution—officers sleeping quarters included.

Where demands are being made which are important enough to warrant drastic action by the group, I.W.W. experience has developed a couple of useful methods applicable to practically any jail. In the case of concrete construction, there is a procedure known as "building a battleship" which involves ten or fifteen men locking arms and standing as close together as possible.. They count, "One, two, three", and on the count of three all jump together. When two or three tons of men land on a small area of floor most buildings feel it. In steel tank jails similar to most county lock-ups, marching in unison around uprights will shake bolts and rivets loose, and can even affect welded construction.

In their relations to the prison population, segregated resisters must remember that a barrier of fear exists between themselves and the conforming inmates, based on the ingenious "pie in the sky" system by which prisoners are coerced into good behavior. The inmate hopes he will make parole when his one-third term expires. Usually, he fails that, since paroles are kept to a percentage established by tradition. No reason is given for this refusal. With hope of parole gone, he looks foward to earning additional "good time" toward earlier release. If unable to do this by working on the prison farm or in prison industry, he still has his conditional release date —earlier than the "full time" date—to hope for. Any infringement of regulations will lose him precious days. These days will be taken away—no specified number for any specified infraction—piecemeal by a special court of officials.

Knowing this fear and uncertainty in the prisoner's mind, the resister relies heavily on humor in attacking the administration. If you can get the inmates to laugh at an officer, half the battle against prison discipline is won.

In one of the Danbury demonstrations, the administration's phoney Christmas spirit was challenged by a large banner strung from the baseball backstop: "FREEDOM IS THE BEST CHRISTMAS GIFT". The slogan appealed to the inmates, and the hacks who were delegated to tear it down met with a roar of disapproval from the crowd, followed by laughter as the wind whipped one end of the banner loose and the guards struggled to get it under control. On another occasion, when the resisters were stirring up feeling about a man locked up in modified solitary, signs were tacked to broom handles, shoved out between the window bars, and unrolled. Inmates returning to quarters from the mess hall stopped to watch while guards placed ladders against the wall and climbed up to snatch the signs. As the uniformed arms stretched out to tear the signs down, however, they were quickly rolled up around the broom handles again and pulled in through the bars, to repeat their performance at another window. The thwarted officers again got the horselaugh.

One elderly guard developed the bad habit of hiding in a recessed doorway beneath our cell block, darting out to pick up messages thrown from the window to other inmates. One of our inventive geniuses took a couple of pieces of toilet tissue, smeared them liberally with stale mustard, wrapped them in another piece of tissue, and tossed them out. The uniform fell for it and elbowed a couple of inmates out of the way in his dash to pick up the "secret message". He got it, all right, and looked mighty silly glancing from his smeared hands to our window.

If you have a lot of time on your hands, an illegal newspaper can be published and distributed with the most primitive equipment. A tin can, milk bottle, or shaped piece of wood, or the sole of a shoe will form a simple mimeograph machine. A piece of blanket will make a mimeograph pad. You can cement it to the tin can etc. with a highly efficient glue made of oatmeal strained through a sock. Stencils and ink may be "borrowed" from the prison office by another inmate. If gelatin can be obtained from the prison kitchen, a duplicator can be made, using any flat container for the gelatin, and an indelible pencil for the master copy, If you can't get paper any other way, do what one of our boys in solitary did: wash the print off magazine pages.

As conditions get tighter, you may find yourself locked securely in individual cells. If there is a half inch of space under the door as there usually is, flat objects may be passed from one cell to another by making a thin rope of tied shoelaces or sheet strips with a weight at one end. This can be skidded across the corridor and under a door on the opposite side. Between floors the ventilating system may be used for talking. Useful things like checkers, chess pieces and so on may be fashioned from a papier maché made of shredded newspapers with oatmeal paste for binder. There are a hundred ways to maintain your morale, and on occasion, to lower that of your opponent. Once, when feeling particularly morose, I cheered myself up by converting three full-size sheets into a pair of rope-soled shoes, and fashioned a medicine ball out of fourteen sets of winter underwear and a laundry bag.

When there are only a tiny handful of resisters, the most dramatic actions are inadvisable.

They may be supplanted by cautious sabotage and the stupidity strike, plus slowdown wherever applicable. The plumbing, lighting and communication systems are vulnerable. Schweikism is the last resort of the individual resister. How much material he may damage in his well-meaning blundering is a matter for the prison book-keeping system.

This matter of the bookkeeping system brings up the angle of getting the drop on an official by uncovering manipulations with the prison budget. In one Federal prison, it was found that a three-way split existed between the warehouse officer, meat dealer and front office. The meat ordered would total 400 pounds. The dealer would deliver 300, but the warehouseman would receipt for the full amount shown on the bill and the front office would pay for it. The take went three ways.

In another prison, a 30' by 25' frame shop with a dirt floor cost $3000 to build with free labor, while a chicken house of cinder block ran to $10,000 with the same free labor. Six inches of sand was dumped on the floor, to be scraped up and thrown out the same year. Irregularities of this sort run through the whole Bureau of Prisons, and it is a rare guard or official who is not lining his pocket with cash or material covered by the jailhouse budget.

The waste which is a unique feature of American economy is sharply evident in prison. Often, food produced on the prison farm will be left on the ground to rot while the men inside the wall belch along on eternal beans and bread pudding. This occurs because prison bookkeeping systems demand that the food from the prison farm be charged against the kitchen at the market price. At Lewisburg Pennitentiary, a large portion of the tomato crop rotted in 1946 because the market price of tomatoes happened to be too high to permit the cons to eat the food they had raised.

Prison is an unhappy parable of life in "outside" society!

THE DANBURY STORY

HOWARD SCHOENFELD

The Warden adjusted his glasses.

"Men," he said, "This is my last appeal to you. Your group is conspiring to buck the authority of the bureau of prisons. If you persist in your foolhardy conspiracy not only your lives, but the lives of the 600 other men in this institution will be adversely affected. So will the lives of the thousands that will follow them. If you won't think of yourselves, think of them. Do you want them to be punished for your actions?"

The Warden paused. His future in the prison system was bound up in his ability to meet such situations as this, and he was doing his best to reason with us. He was a man of about fifty, with a clean cut, intelligent face.

His position was both delicate and difficult. If word of our impending strike reached the public there would, undoubtedly, be a terrific reaction to it, and he was certain to be made the scapegoat. On the other hand if word failed to reach the public he would probably be accused of suppressing the news, and meanwhile his authority within the prison seemed sure to be undermined.

The Warden was a man with a comparatively advanced outlook. There were adequate recreational facilities in his prison, smoking was permitted in the mess hall, movies were shown once a week, inmates were allowed to put on shows, the yard period was long, the institution's soft ball team was given ample time to practice, and the prison generally was run along what are considered liberal lines.

The Warden was a good natured man with a sense of humor and a keen feeling of sympathy for the underdog. Ironically, he requested the prison bureau to send us to his prison; and, to be perfectly honest, the worst we suffered under his administration was solitary confinement, whereas wardens at other prisons allowed guards to beat and torture inmates of our type.

The Warden was a sports enthusiast of the first order. No broadcast of a fight or an important game passed without the inmates hearing it. He had been known to rouse the whole prison after lights out to show a new fight film, even going so far as to let the men in solitary out to see it. And no inmate was happier than he over the fact that the prison soft ball team was undefeated in a really excellent league, and was scheduled to play the other undefeated team, a group of college men, in a few weeks, for the championship of that area.

The prison team's high standing was due to the good pitching of a convict in our group of strikers, and it was this, coupled with the Warden's love of sports, that was partially responsible for the extraordinary event which occured in the prison later.

The Warden was a liberal with a position of authority in an evil system. On the whole he attempted to use his authority to alleviate the evil. The attempt was foredoomed and futile. Despite everything he had done, his prison was still a hell on earth.

Negroes were segregated, teen aged convicts were thrown into solitary, foul food was served frequently, the lunacy ward was used to coerce the sane, reading matter was censored unmercifully, stool pigeons plied their rotten trade, men 'blew their tops', and the constant surveillance and grinding monotony of confinement took its inevitable toll.

The reforms instituted by the Warden seemed to us to be of

a piddling nature when placed alongside the general horror of everyday prison life, through we weren't striking against the prison system at that time. Many of us had clashed with the system and would continue to do so, but on this occasion our strike was of a more fundamental nature.

Inescapably, the Warden was forced to oppose us, and uphold his authority; and, with it, the authority of the evil system that gave him his power. For a kind man, which he seemed to me to be, it was a tragic situation.

A good impulse prompted him to ask the prison bureau to send us to his prison. His fate was to discover us unmanageable. We were a proud, stiff-necked lot who openly boasted we were the most radical men in the country. We lined up that way, radical versus liberal, and began our struggle.

The Warden continued to speak.

"If you carry through with this strike, not only will your lives be affected, but liberalism itself may be wiped out in the prison bureau. All of you know how hard some of us in the bureau have struggled to better the lot of the inmate. We've made progress lately, and we expect to make more, but the forces against us are powerful, and the balance delicate. A strike at this time may upset the balance and throw the prison bureau backwards to the conditions of 20 years ago. None of you men want that."

"But we aren't striking against the prison bureau," someone said.

"It doesn't make any difference why you're striking. The question is can any group in a federal prison call a strike at any time. The issue here is whether your group of twenty or thirty men has the authority in this prison or whether the people of the United States through the Federal Bureau of Prisons and the Warden have it."

The Warden was good humored and even friendly despite the forcefulness of his words.

"I want to be fair to you men," he said. "In many ways the circumstances behind this strike are unusual, and therefore I'm willing to make concessions. For example I might allow your group to cease work on the designated day and turn the chapel over to you, provided you give your word not to ask the rest of the inmate body to join you. You'll have to make it clear, however, that you're not protesting against the prison bureau and that the nature of the services are religious, rather than a strike.

The fairness of this proposal struck me at once and I was genuinely sorry we couldn't agree with the Warden on it. Unfortunately, any arrangement other than a strike would have destroyed the meaning and effect of our protest.

"Any inmate who wants to join us has been invited to do so," a convict said.

The Warden shook his head.

"Impossible. Supposing everybody joins you. Who will man the hospitals and take care of the sick? Who will take care of the kitchen and other chores?"

"We'll leave skeleton crews on duty," another convict said.

"None of the other inmates are going to join us, anyway," someone else said.

Others chipped in with similar comments.

The Warden raised his hand for silence.

"I've made my offer," he said. "It's up to you to decide whether you'll take it or not. If not, you'll have to take the consequences."

We decided to take the consequences.

The other inmates, though they failed to join the strike, kept us informed and-or misinformed via the grapevine of the Prison Bureau's moves the following day.

The Bureau, thoroughly aroused, acted swiftly.

Apparently fearing a general strike of riot proportions, carloads of Department of Justice men, armed with machine guns and tear gas, were unloaded at the prison gates, according to the grapevine. Other Department of Justice men, it seemed, were released in the prison disguised as inmates. Guards, on their own hook, and probably without official knowledge, went their rounds letting the inmates know they'd be safe in starting fights with any in our group of conscientious objectors, if they wanted to do so. Our case as pacifists would be less clear in the public eye if we fought back, thereby making it possible for the Bureau to get tougher with us.

Early in the afternoon stool pigeons began circulating among the men in an effort to bring inmate pressure to bear on us. The prison would be punished as a whole if the strike took place, they explained. Smoking, letter writing, and visiting privileges would be withdrawn from all. Other punitive measures would be taken.

The six or seven hundred bootleggers, counterfeiters, embezzlers, smugglers, pimps, white slavers, con men, dope peddlers, robbers, murderers, and what have you, comprising the so-called criminal population of the prison stood to lose considerably by our strike; yet not one of them put the slightest pressure on us to change our stand.

During the few months we had been in prison the inmates had grown to love and respect us—as we had them. They were a patient, forebearing body, daily putting up with the most degrading and despicable treatment by the prison bureau. We cast our lot in with theirs from the beginning, and all of our group of ministers, divinity students, and socialists had been in solitary or restrictions at one time or another for protesting against the evil conditions under which they lived.

Furthermore, in our group of absolutists, were many spiritually developed men of almost saintly stature. Even the judges who sentenced them recognized it. One judge, after hearing the Union Theological Seminary students in our group, wept and apologized as he passed sentence on them. Another judge, sentencing Arle Brooks, after reviewing his life of service to others in a probationary report, remarked that he felt like Pontius Pilate.

These men and the others seemed to me, a socialist, to be the first truly religious men I had ever met, and I have known rabbis, ministers, priests, and church goers all my life. Under their influence many an inmate, who had never known kindness or even decent treatment before, discovered his own spiritual potential.

The guards and prison officials were also aware of the unusual situation in the prison, and more than one commented on it. There was less swearing, fighting and sex talk; more studying, discussion and quiet re-appraisement. A general restoration of self respect seemed to be taking place among the men.

Our strike was one in which they had no apparent stake; yet they were as zealous of our welfare as if they had been blood relatives.

By late afternoon the prison was in a state of nervous apprehension. When the supper whistle blew that evening the men poured out of their cell blocks and surged across the prison yard toward the mess hall, carrying us along with them. Midway, they came to a sudden halt.

The Warden was standing on a small box in the center of the yard. Guards quickly rounded the men up and herded them into a bunched mass in front of him. Other convicts continued to pour out into the mob. I moved toward the rear and two guards detached themselves and moved in behind me. Other guards stationed themselves wherever there were conscientious objectors. The men stirred restlessly, anxious to get to their suppers. Night was falling and a high wind was whipping through the yard.

The Warden began to speak.

As everyone knew, he said, a general strike was being called the next morning by a small group of inmates. The nature of the strike as he saw it did not concern the rest of the inmates and he expressed the belief that they wouldn't join us. We were not striking against the Prison Bureau or the administration of the prison, he pointed out, but against the government of the U.S.

The patriotism of the group calling the strike, though we were not yet at war, was of a questionable nature. We had deliberately disobeyed the law of the land and that was why we were in prison. We had been trouble makers from the beginning and now we were wilfully calling a strike against the best interests of the nation.

Everybody was against war, including himself, and he had gone along with us as long as he could, offering to allow us the use of the chapel for prayer and meditation on the designated day, but we had rejected the offer, preferring to flout the authority of the prison bureau and the government.

The selfishness of our course was apparent. A strike in the prison bureau at this time might prove disastrous. The Bureau was more liberal than at any time in its history. He dwelt on the gains that had been made recently and emphasized the benefits accruing to the inmates. Our strike would be a blow to those gains, giving the reactionary opposition an opportunity to criticize, and halt them, possibly destroy them altogether. The inmates would see the wisdom of steering clear of our strike, and the selfishness of it. He expressed his confidence in the men, and knew he could count on them for support. He paused for applause.

Silence met him.

Hastily, he continued his speech. He emphasized again the gains that had been made in the bureau, the threat to them, the selfishness of our group of men. We had so little consideration for the inmates we were going to deprive them of their food, if we had our way, by calling the kitchen help out on strike. We were going to deprive the hospital of help, leaving the sick and dying to shift for themselves. The Warden was interrupted by a clear, but respectful voice.

"That's not quite true, Warden."

The speaker was Arle Brooks, a minister of the Disciples of Christ, known among the men for his meek character and spiritual humility.

The Warden focussed his attention on Arle.

"Seize that man," he said, pointing at him.

Guards quickly surrounded Arle, locking their arms together around him.

The inmates, knowing Arle's character, broke into spontaneous laughter at the unnesessary precaution. The laughter died instantly when the Warden ordered Arle taken away and thrown into solitary.

A wave of angry muttering swept through the crowd.

The Warden demanded silence and went on with his speech. The muttering continued ominously. The Warden quickly ended on a patriotic note, got off his box, and staying close to his guards disappeared into one of the buildings. Guards shoved the men across the yard toward the mess hall. The muttering continued.

After supper we circulated among the men as much as possible, attempting to quiet them. By lights out, the prison was somewhat calmer. I was quartered in an inside steel wire enclosed space, called a medium custody dormitory by the prison officials. The floors were concrete and the small area was enclosed by concrete walls. In it were eight or nine crowded rows of steel cots on which the men slept. Between the steel wire and the back wall was a small walk along which guards made their nightly rounds. In the dead of night I was aroused by a guard carrying a flashlight. He shook me awake.

"Get your clothes and follow me."

I picked my way through the mass of sleeping men and followed him into an adjoining room where I was allowed to dress. Speech was forbidden. After a long wait a guard came down the cat walk leading two other conscientious objectors. We followed them silently down the corridor through the maze of the prison. I had no idea what was in store for us, but knowing the prison bureau, I had no doubt that it was going to be unpleasant. We emerged in front of a large waiting room. Inside were the other men of our group, sitting silently. We went in and took our places with them. I lit a cigarette. A guard took it from me. The clock on the wall ticked.

A Lieutenant of guards entered and checked our names against the list he was carrying. He disappeared down the corridor, suddenly; and, as suddenly, reappeared. He read a name.

"David Dellinger."

Dave arose and followed him. David was a divinity student whose first act in prison had been against the segregation of Negroes. Walking into the mess hall he had deliberately stepped out of the white men's line and sat at a Negro table. The mess hall is the most heavily guarded spot in a prison and the simple action took extreme courage. His punishment was swift and ruthless; yet afterwards, he had consistently opposed the Bureau's racist policy along with the rest of us. Outside, he had done settlement work in slums, while still attending Theological Seminary. Previously, he had held an English exchange scholarship which, in the religious world, parallels the Rhodes Scholarship. He failed to return.

We waited. The guards watched. The silence was heavy, broken only by the ticking of the clock. The sound of footsteps, coming from the distant end of the corridor, reached us. The Lieutenant arrived at the door, entered, and looked at his list.

"Sturge Steinert," he said.

Steinert arose and followed him. We listened as the echo of dual footsteps receded in the corridor and faded out. Steinert was a socialist who had been a student at Temple University. The American Legion had awarded him a scholarship for winning an essay contest on Americanism. The scholarship, I believe, was withdrawn when he carried his ideals into practice. He also failed to return.

The Lieutenant entered and read another name.

"Gordon Goley."

Goley was a religious man who had renounced all things material, and devoted his full time to a study of the Bible. Independently, through prayer and meditation, he had attained a spiritual stature as yet unachieved by most western religionists. His unaffected simplicity and truly holy character were a source of inspiring strength, and his mere presence in any group was a powerful agent for good. In the ancient meaning of the term, he was, and is, probably the only living holy man in the United States.

He too, failed to return.

The Lieutenant called for us, one by one. The wait, for those of us who were not at the top of the list, seemed interminable. I became extremely nervous. I looked around the room at the men waiting with me, for reassurance.

They were the finest people I had ever known. Gathered up from everywhere they seemed to me to embody the conscience of America. Each could have obtained his release from prison instantly by registering in the draft, and nearly all, being ministers and divinity students, would have been automatically exempted from service. The rest, for one reason or another, would also have been free at that time. Each in his own way had led an exemplary life, and I was proud to be associated with them.

Eventually, the Lieutenant entered and called my name. I arose and followed him. Walking down the corridor, I remember being amused by the situation, and for the moment, enjoying the sensation of participating in a comic opera. The reality of the waiting Lord High Executioner destroyed the brief pleasantry.

At the end of the corridor I was frisked before being led through the steel barred door that opened into a section of the prison that was devoted to administration offices. The Lieutenant opened the door to the Warden's office, and motioned me to enter.

I had had the sensation of being in comic opera, but the sensation now on entering the Warden's office, was that of stepping into an Arabian Night's adventure.

For months we had seen nothing in the way of furniture or decoration except steel cots, metal chairs, and concrete walls. The Warden's office, by contrast, seemed luxurious. Furnished with thick rugs, modern furniture, invitingly deep chairs, and an abundance of wall pictures, the comparative splendor of the room momentarily dazzled me.

Incongruously, the Warden completed the picture. Apparently having left a social function to return to the prison, he was still wearing full dress evening clothes, the coat of which he had discarded in favor of a smoking jacket. He was sitting at his desk, a volume of poetry in one hand, while, with the other, he tuned a station in on his desk radio. The luxury of his office coupled with his, for a prison, bizarre dress had the effect of sharply emphasizing the differences in our positions.

The Warden invited me to be seated and, to my astonishment asked me had I read Walt Whitman's "Leaves of Grass", which he had in his hand. His manner was friendly and disarming though he continued to manipulate the dial of the radio nervously throughout the interview. He expressed his regret that he hadn't had the opportunity to discuss my viewpoint with me previously and hoped when I was released we could meet on more social terms over a glass of beer. I returned the polite sentiment. He went on to show his interest in my reasons for joining in the present strike, and I showed him a copy of a note I had given earlier to the Captain of guards, stating my motives. He read the short note, which, as I remember it, went something like this:

"As an expression of solidarity with the student peace strike outside, the majority of the people of the United States, and countless millions throughout the world, I intend to refuse to work on April 23, 1941. I am not striking against the U.S. government or the Bureau of Prisons, but against war, which I believe to be the greatest evil known to man."

The Warden brought the interview to a close a few minutes later and called the Lieutenant of guards who led me away, and threw me into solitary confinement.

A friendly guard explained to me later that a dictaphone was concealed in the Warden's office, connected with his radio, and that transcripts of his interviews with each of us were made and sent to Washington. What the purpose was, I cannot imagine.

Solitary confinement was referred to as 'constructive meditation' by the prison authorities. It differed in no way, insofar as I know, from solitary confinement anywhere. Men went in, endured the terrifying ordeal, and came out weakened, sometimes dulled and apathetic for months or years afterwards, and sometimes broken altogether. During my stay in prison at least one man attempted suicide in solitary preferring death to the barbaric torture.

My cell measured five of my paces long and two wide. The walls and floor were bare concrete. The door was metal with a small glass square built in it. Guards spied in on me from time to time. Owing to our number, a new cell block, not ordinarily used for solitary purposes had to be opened up, and the advantage was that light seeped in to us through glass apertures. Strict silence was maintained, though I soon discovered I could get a response from George Houser, who was in the next cell by pounding on the wall.

The first day dragged uneventfully, the second monotonously, the third worse. I paced my cell for hours on end, throwing myself on my cot exhausted, and losing myself in daydreams. Insatiable sexual desires overwhelmed me, and I lost count of the days in the interminable silence, which was broken only by the dull voice of the guard during count. I began to look forward to mealtimes when an inmate, prevented from talking to me by the presence of a guard, deposited a tray inside the cell. One evening I found a cigarette and match neatly taped on the underside of the tray. Delighted, I smoked it to the end, burning my fingers, becoming dizzy and nauseated on the smoke.

The days passed. I made up songs and listened to the words in my head. I wrote mental essays, novels, plays and short stories. I scratched my growing beard and braided my hair to while away the time. I reviewed my life, picking out the incidents I liked best and dwelling on them endlessly. I thought about god and prayed. I pounded the wall and paced the cell. One day I began screaming mad parodies of patriotic music at the top of my lungs, and brought a guard scurrying down the corridor to my cell. I told him I'd been bit by a patriot and had caught patriotic fever. He grinned at me and told me to shut up. I fell on my cot and laughed at my own joke.

More than anything I longed to hear a voice, not dully counting but saying something with feeling in it, a speech, a polite conversation, a political discussion, or even a poetry recitation.

I got my wish on the calmest and quietest day of all, a Sunday when not a sound of any kind was audible in the cell block. Unexpectedly, Ernest Kirkjian, an ascetic of Armenian descent, began to sing the Latin version of Ave Maria. The holy music sounded incredibly beautiful after the awful days of silence, and it seemed to me I was hearing, really hearing and feeling, the human voice in its true splendor for the first time. The saintliness and purity of angels seemed to me to be in Kirkjian's song, and something profound and hitherto untouched inside me, went out and mingled with it.

The song ended, and down the corridor, Bill Lovell began to intone the Lord's prayer. The other Christians joined in and recited it, and Al Herling, Stan Rappaport and myself joined together and recited an ancient Hebrew prayer.

It was a good day.

Weeks passed.

One day a guard entered the cell block, walked down the corridor and opened the door to Benedict's cell. Benedict, like most of the pacifists in our group, was a fine athlete. Outside, his physical prowess was a legend in amateur athletic circles, and, in particular, he excelled as a soft ball pitcher. Big muscled, strong and agile, his speed ball was so swift only one man in the prison could catch him. The prison team, built around his pitching, was tied for first place in its league, and his ability to hold the opposition scoreless had placed it there. The inmates, probably for the first time in the history of prison ball, were solidly behind their team, which originally entered the league expecting to serve as a scrub practise team for the other amateurs in that area.

The Warden, a sports lover, was delighted with the unusual situation, and it did not surprise us to hear the guard offer Benedict his freedom if he would pitch the championship play-off games, which were scheduled for that day. Benedict pointed out he was in no condition to pitch after his long confinement, and wasn't sure he could make it. The guard explained he would be given time to limber up and mentioned how disappointed the inmates would be if the championship was lost. Benedict thereupon said he would do it. He added, however, only on condition that all the men in solitary, including the inmates not in the pacifist group, were released, The guard said he would speak to the Warden about it, and we heard him trudge down the corridor.

We waited in silence till he came back. The Warden could not agree to Benedict's terms, but he offered a compromise. He would release all the conscientious objectors for the game, and Benedict permanently. Benedict refused. The guard disappeared, returning shortly thereaftar with another offer. The Warden would release everybody for the game, and Benedict permanently. Benedict refused. The Guard disappeared.

About a half hour later a Lieutenant of guards entered and told Benedict the men were warming up for the first game. The inmates, he said, were aware of his refusal to pitch, and were resentful towards him and the rest of us. He then said he thought he could prevail on the Warden to release all the conscientious objectors permanently, and the other men in solitary for the game, if Benedict would do it. Benedict refused.

Fully an hour passed before the Captain of guards entered and released us. The prison team had lost the first game of the series, and the Warden, unable to endure further losses, had agreed to Benedict's terms.

Grinning hugely, we left our cells, and laughing at each other's pasty complexions, bearded faces, and unkempt hair, hurried out into the prison yard. A wave of applause went through the inmate stands as Benedict rushed down the field and began warming up.

Benedict, in true Frank Merriwell fashion, summoned his strength after the long weeks of demoralized living, and, in a superhuman and prodigious performance, pitched batter after batter out, enabling the prison team to rally and score, and win the series.

Word of the remarkable feat reached the neighboring cities through the sports pages of their newspapers, and later, when Benedict was released, over 20,000 people paid fancy admission prices to see him in action at a benefit game.

Morale broke down completely in the prison after the games,

when we were rounded up, including Benedict, and thrown back into solitary. The guard on duty was so disgusted he did not even bother to lock our cells.

The next day at noon the Warden reversed his stand and released us. The midday whistle had blown and the men were already in the mess hall, eating. We straggled across the empty yard, basking in the sun, enjoying our freedom. A spontaneous wave of applause broke out among the men as the first of our group entered the hall. Surging across the hall the wave became a crescendo. Six hundred pairs of hands joined in and the crescendo became pandemonium. Guards ran up and down the aisles; they were ignored. The pandemonium increased when Benedict entered the hall, maintaining itself at an incredible pitch. A volcano of thunderous and deafening applause burst out when Arle Brooks entered, but when the so-called criminals who had been in solitary came in, the convicts literally went wild, beating their metal cups on the tables, and stamping their feet.

We stood in the center of the hall, astounded at the demonstration. It became clear to me that although they were applauding Benedict, Brooks, and all of us who had been in solitary, they were doing something more. A mass catharsis of human misery was taking place before our eyes. Some of the men were weeping, others were laughing like madmen. It was like nothing I had ever seen before, and nothing I ever expect to see again.

Men went in, endured the terrifying ordeal and came out weakened, sometimes dulled and apathetic for months or years...

A FIELD OF BROKEN STONES[+]

LOWELL NAEVE

July, 1941

The days in quarantine—the first, the second, the rest—went pretty much the same—

The first thing we heard in the morning was a bugle sharply calling out reveille. Next there were sounds of keys—a key opening the quarantine door. There were sounds of a guard shuffling about inside the cell block, laying his brief case and keys on a table, hanging up his coat.

We stayed in our bunks, waited. We heard more jangling of keys, then a key turning the lock of a lever box. The door squeaked as it opened. I imagined the guard peering into the box to see that all the dials and levers were "just right". He'd take ahold of a lever; the long steel arms above our doors scraped, fell into place. The moment was near......

......A shrilling piercing whistle. It entered every cell, filled the void between the opposite tiers. The echoes of the shrill died out, the cell block seemed cold and hollow. A curt command: EVERYBODY UP! Our cell doors slid open simultaneously. Like

[+] From the book of this title, written by Lowell Naeve in collaboration with David Wieck, and published by the Libertarian Press.

everyone else, I looked through my open door at the tiers of of cells across the way. Everyone was getting up.

We didn't want to get up, but we did. Why? We didn't know......We just got up. Behind me and behind every man hung one vague doubt: if we didn't do what we were told, what would they do to us? There was the "hole"; various stories and descriptions of it were going the rounds. If the authorities put us in the hole, in solitary, for a couple of months, would we be able to take it?

There was, as it seemed to me, this big question mark. So—everyone got up, everyone did as he was told.

When the guard said, "O. K. boys, let's mop up," we mopped up. If the guard said "Let's clean the brass", we cleaned the brass; it made no difference if the brass was clean and we felt it could be made no cleaner. If the guard said "O.K., line up," we lined up. That's all there was to it. Dictatorially prisons are run; by threat the men are ruled.

The only thing that kept each individual, including myself, from feeling completely stupid and ridiculous was that he saw everyone doing the same and obeying the same as he did.

When we went to eat we were made to line up to get our food, told where and how to sit down. After breakfast, which was very poor, we were sent out to work on the yard gang. The yard was the square that the surrounding dull-yellow buildings enclosed. The prison had no walls as such—the smooth-faced buildings were themselves the walls; they looked high and unclimbable.

The prison was only a few months old. The yard was a good deal the way the construction company had left it. The yard was barren and bleak; there was nothing in it but uneven broken mounds of yellow clay.

The yard gang was already at work. The yard-boss, a tall sturdy-built guard, dryly motioned us over to a pile of well-worn picks and shovels. We were lined up, told what to do. The yellow clay was baked and hard, full of stones. Very shortly the other prisoners informed me that picking was, for the most part, "just to keep us busy."

As I went through the motions of working, following the mind and wishes of the guard, I struggled with my emotions. I wanted to use my time constructively. I disliked being pushed around but I decided to say nothing for awhile—maybe something would happen. At times it felt as though my growing disgust was going to rise out of my stomach and speak of itself.

We picked till noon. We were taken to eat. We picked all afternoon till 4:30, then we were, with the rest of the prison, locked up and counted. Shortly after the count we were given food again. The rest of the evening and the night we were kept in quarantine.

Each day the prison's dictatorial regimentation was grinding into me more and more. We weren't supposed to think, just supposed to do and obey. Each command was a threat—we did as told, or else!

After breakfast on the fifth day I was given a new assignment, told to go with a guard. They didn't ask me, just told me to go—it was assumed I would go.

I went with the guard, said nothing......Inside me was a rising feeling I could hardly suppress. With some other prisoners I followed the guard across the yard. I was completely disgusted with myself for obeying. I knew as I followed the guard that sooner or later I would have to balk at being dictated to.

I looked ahead at the walk. Twenty feet foward was a spot. I looked at the spot, and I knew I was going to stop. I grew warm all over. I felt a gathering of my loose emotions. I reached the spot, stopped.

The guard and the other prisoners reached the green door they were headed for. The guard turned, counted his men. He noticed me standing in the walk about forty feet back.

"Hey, you!" he yelled, "Come on!" I said nothing. "Hey!" he yelled, "What's the matter?" He waited a bit, then walked towards me. "What's the matter?"

"I can't go any farther."

"What do you mean?"

"I can't go any farther."

"What do you mean?"

"I won't go any farther."

He broke in: "You mean you refuse to work?"

"You can call it what you want, I don't care......It's just... I want to have some say how my life is to be run. I'm tired of being dictated to."

He acted as though he didn't hear me. "Are you coming along?"

"No."

"Well, we'll see about that."

He took me over to a cell house in the corner of the yard. I wondered what was going to happen, but I didn't particularly care. With another guard, he marched me up past three tiers of barred cells, locked me in a top cell.

In the cell I felt relieved. The burning growl inside of me was gone. I had opposed what I thought wrong. For the first time in a month I felt sure and collected.

In a few minutes a young prisoner came to the front of my cell. He rested his elbows on the bars, and in a very friendly voice said: "You're Naeve, the new war objector?" I said yes. He enthusiastically extended his hand through the bars: "I'm one, too; Schoenfeld's the name."

In a soft voice he asked me what had happened. We talked awhile. He left, saying: "I'll be back. If there's anything you need, tell me. I'll get it for you."

An hour passed. A guard came, marched me over to the prison hospital, locked me up in an observation cell. There was nothing in the cell but a bed, nothing to read or occupy my time.

......The thought came vividly to mind: They were trying to frighten me with being put in the hole or being shipped to Springfield, Missouri. "Springfield" was, I heard, the federal prison-hospital where prisoners were often intimidated and roughed up If you are sent there, it implies you are crazy.

......How long would they keep me in the cell? How long

could I stand it? I walked up and down. From time to time I noticed faces peering in through the cell-door's small shatterproof window.

The large window opposite the cell door had no vent. The July sun shone in. By 10:30 the cell was stifling hot.

At twelve o'clock the cell door was opened and a tray of food was set in. Then from time to time in the afternoon there would be a knock at my cell door. A prisoner would motion in the little glass window, then talk to me through the crack between the door and the door-jamb. They all said pretty much the same: "Take it easy kid. You're right to buck them, but you can't beat the system." Then in a friendly way: "Why don't you give it up? Why don't you do like everybody else? You're doing it the hard way."

I contrasted their feelings with mine. They were, it appeared, doing it the hardest way. They were depressed and disgusted with themselves for doing what they didn't want to do. I felt comparatively free.

One day passed, then two. I took to walking back and forth, to facilitate my thinking. Doing nothing but thinking was, I discovered, amazingly enjoyable. I thought a good deal of Madeline, those I knew back home. I thought a good deal about equality—that I, as a human being, had a right, an inalienable right, to equality. No man was above me, no man was below me. I thought about the right to run my own life. I had occasionally thought of these things when free. Now I thought of them a good deal.

The third day—nothing happened.

On the fourth day at 7 p.m. I heard a key in my door. Surprised, I looked up. A short pear-shaped man in carefree slacks walked briskly into the cell. He smiled, made motions he wanted to shake my hand. We shook hands. "Hello, Naeve, I'm Warden Gerlach."

He paused, grinned. "How are you getting along?" He moved over to the low cell-window, sat on the window-ledge, adjusted his horn-rimmed glasses. In a serious tone: "What's the matter, Naeve, what's the matter?"

"I think I ought to have some say about how my own life is to be run...... I want to do some physical work three or four hours a day to keep in good shape. But the rest of the time I want to study and paint......I'd just like to be left alone to paint my own things."

He looked out of the window awhile. "I think that can be arranged. We can probably set aside a fund of fifty dollars or so for art materials."

I didn't want to feel obligated to Mr. Gerlach. I told him that I preferred to have paints sent in from outside, pay for them myself. He agreed.

"Would you be willing to go back to quarantine and stay there till your paints arrive?" I said I would. "Is there anything else you want?"

"I'd like to get out of jail."

He laughed, the conversation shifted. After twenty minutes of casual talk, he left. He seemed pleased with the visit and the bargain he'd made.

The next day back in quarantine I began thinking about the warden's $50 proposal. It puzzled me. Most of the men in quarantine didn't even have socks to wear. The warden's cry was the institution didn't have funds.

In the remaining three weeks of quarantine I came to know many of the prisoners. Two were new war objectors. One of the objectors, Gene Garst, was a tall sharp-featured merchant seaman from Philadelphia. Gene, in a long speech in court, had advocated everyone leaving the army, to curb the trend toward war. For this he was given the limit—five years.

The other objector, "Scotty", was a very cheerful insurance salesman, married just a short while. His wife was expecting a baby.

A month passed. For some of us, quarantine period was over. We were given regular prison clothes—white undershirt and shorts, white socks, one pair of light-blue trousers, an army belt, one light-blue shirt. "You'll get a change of clothes once a week."

At the same time my paints arrived. The warden, enthusiastically: "I've arranged it so you can use one of the dressing rooms in the auditorium as a "studio". It'll be a good place to paint."

August-September, 1941.

One afternoon while I was painting in "the studio", Warden Gerlach came in to visit me. We began talking about an idea I had for a mural based on Van Loon's book, The Story of Mankind. It ended up, Mr. Gerlach told me he had some decorating in his home he'd like done. He broached the idea he wanted a portrait of one of his children—and later possibly one of himself. The other prisoners had warned me this would happen. So I explained the procedure I had in mind.

I told him I believed in equality. Prisoners had also asked me to do portraits. I suggested that we might put cards for the prisoners and others interested, in a hat. We could draw a card—whosever card it was, I'd paint their portrait first.

The warden seemed a little taken aback that his request would have to wait its democratic turn.

The warden came to see me several times while I was painting. Guards frequently dropped in for a chat. Their visits took up much of my time. After a few weeks I decided I would have to do something about the visits so I could get some work done. The warden had agreed I was to be left alone, but it wasn't working out that way.

One day after I entered the workshop I put up two easels to bar the entrance, put a sign on the easels, went to work.

An hour passed...... I heard the voices of Mr Gerlach and several elderly women coming toward the workshop door. He had brought the women up from the city of Danbury to show them the prison (I was part of the exhibit). Mr. Gerlach and the women were approaching the door. I somewhat froze.

I tried to keep on working just as before. The door began

to swing open. Mr. Gerlach was opening it in a very patronizing manner. He gestured toward me, not quite looking, and said: "And here we have a young man, Mr. Naeve, who is..." He paused. The five elderly women were reading the sign.

The sign read: "I want to work. Would you please leave me alone?" And then down below in small letters: "This positively includes the President of the United States." The latter was jokingly put in so that Mr. Gerlach and the guards would know I wasn't referring just to prisoners.

The old women finished looking at the sign. They looked up at me through the easels that barred the door, giggled, stopped short their giggles, looked at the sign again. They didn't know what to do or how to act. They looked toward the Warden.

Mr Gerlach looked at me. He seemed puzzled, he seemed confident, then he seemed embarrassed. Half-confidently he said, peering through the easel bars: "Would you......would you, Mr. Naeve, like to show us some of your paintings?"

I felt a little uneasy. I hesitated to answer, thought it over, then said, slowly and seriously: "No, I don't believe I'd care to."

Mr. Gerlach, not looking too perplexed, nor too confident, closed the door, escorted the women away. I felt I had said the right thing. I hadn't helped the Warden create the impression, This is how I treat all the boys.

I began to pack up my things. I thought to myself, This is the end of the painting. But nothing happened. A day or two later Mr. Gerlach left on his vacation.

While the warden was on vacation, I came to know one of the other war objectors well. Al Hurling had been set up with a piano in the auditorium next to the workshop. Al was an exceptional pianist. He was one half of Mr. Gerlach's exhibit, I the second.

The month Mr. Gerlach was gone, Al and I did considerable work. Al practiced and composed, I painted. But when Mr. Gerlach returned, the whole prison took on an air of tension; it was back on needles and pins.

Two or three days passed, when Captain Thieman, a guard

and myself were called into Mr. Gerlach's office. My eye followed the plush soft rug on the office floor, the comfortable chairs, the cheerful curtains at the windows.

We no more than sat down and Mr Gerlach began to tell me what he'd like to have me paint. He had several posters in mind. "Now, the first one," he began, "you make it like this......" He leaned over the desk a way; with his short chubby hands he drew hurriedly how he wanted me to do it. "The second one—I would like to have it made this way." He leaned over again, drew out the plan for the second poster, looked up to see if I understood. He then quickly went on to the third and fourth posters.

When he had finished explaining, he turned to the guard: "Give Naeve whatever materials he needs to do this work." He then turned to Captain Thieman: "You'll see that the orders are made up for these things, and see that he gets the necessary passes for the carpenter shop?" Mr. Thieman nodded.

Mr. Gerlach looked at me, asked did I have it clear in mind what he wanted?

It appeared he thought he could use me whichever way he wanted. He acted as if he owned my life. I recalled the promise he had made to leave me alone to do my own work.

As calmly as I could I replied: "I don't think I'll do it."

The two guards stood like stone. There was an air of breathless silence, a pause. Mr. Gerlach jumped up from his chair, barked demandingly:

"What do you mean, you don't think you'll do it?"

Mr. Gerlach, I thought, was acting like a dictator. I didn't think there was anything I could say. I got up from the chair and walked out of the office into the yard.

During the afternnoon guards notified me several times that the Warden wanted to see me. I wasn't sure what was best to do but I was so riled up that I told them I didn't care to go.

The next day an order came out: I was to work on the pick-and-shovel gang all day, and not at painting. I remembered the previous bargain that I was to have a place to paint, so I paid no attention to the order, continued painting.

A week passed, then one day I met Mr. Gerlach outside the workshop. When he saw I was about to enter, he said commandingly: "I thought I told you to stay out of there." In sinking disgust, remembering our bargain, I said: "That's right", and walked on past him into the shop. The warden started off at a fast pace for the front office.

In a few minutes a guard arrived, told me to pack my materials. As ordered, I carried the supplies to the steps of the front office, left them there.

I walked towards close custody cell house. I couldn't work in the prison at a regular job. In doing prison work we were only building and maintaining a prison to keep ourselves in. I couldn't see the logic to that.

I walked into the cell house. The guard on duty followed me as I headed for my cell. "What are you doing, coming in from work at this time?" I told him I had made up my mind to do the remainder of my time in the cell. The space was small, but in it I could live somewhat the way *I wanted*. I could get up when I wanted, I could walk when I wanted, I could read, study and draw. I wouldn't have to lead the ridiculous regimented routine of the prison.

After the guards had locked me into my cell, I wrote a note to Warden Gerlach, telling him I preferred to live in a cell; I wanted as little to do with the prison as possible; all I asked was to be left alone.

The guard on duty took my note out to the front office. An hour later I heard several guards and the Chief Medical Officer approaching on the tier-walk. They stopped in front of my cell. Doc Sturgell called out: "What's the matter, Naeve?"

I answered that I did not care to get into a discussion with them about it. "I sent in a note of explanation to Mr Gerlach, the rest is up to him."

Then one of the three guards asked the same question. I said nothing, it was no use. It would only lead to ridicule.

When the guards saw I wasn't going to argue with them they went down to the end lock-box, pulled the levers, opened my barred gate. A chill went down my spine. I decided to concentrate all on creating one impression—that I just wanted to be left alone.

I could hear the guards and doctor coming back down the tier-walk. They would soon enter the cell. I took the most casual position I could. I sat on my bunk, legs crossed, and began looking at some reproductions of paintings I had clipped from old magazines.

The cell was very small; the guards were right on top of me when they entered. They asked me more questions. I never looked up. As casually as I could, I kept turning the pictures. The air appeared to be full of guard-anger that couldn't find a way to turn itself loose. They kept questioning, trying to get me into an argument. I said nothing.

"O.K., Naeve, come along, we're taking you out of here."

I had decided to refuse to do everything. It was the only way to eventually being left alone. I remained sitting on the bed.

Finally one of the guards grabbed at one of my hands. I drew it away from him. Then two grabbed at at my arms, began pulling me out of the cell. At that moment I had only one thought in my mind—RELAX. I crumpled to the floor. The guards, fearing something had happened, stopped where they were.

The third guard looked at the drooped body from outside the cage, gasped in: "What's the matter with him?" Doc Sturgell, who had also stepped back: "I don't know." Then he took a good look at me, said, seemingly surprised at the thought: "I think he's doing what they call passive resistance. Let go of him; let's see." The two guards let go, stepped back. I got up and sat on the bed, began looking at the pictures again.

The guards went out of the cell, conferred. I overheard one say: "Guess we'll have to carry him."

They came into the cell a second time, grabbed. I relaxed, slumped. Two guards took hold of my legs. The other grabbed me below the shoulders from behind. The doctor sort of oversaw the operation.

A cold sickening feeling came into my stomach. There is something disgusting about someone taking your body and against your will carrying it off.

I felt like four separate parts. Each leg-end and arm-end seemed very far out from me. They didn't feel attached. One guard took fairly short steps, another long steps. Each part moved in a different rhythm.

When they reached the head of the stairs that led to the first floor, they paused. It would be difficult to carry the relaxed body down the narrow spiral stairway. They discussed it a bit. I was getting heavier, they decided to start right away.

After the difficult turning in the narrow stairway, we came to the narrow cell-house door. The guard in front put my legs down, grabbed for the door. It was locked! The guard who held my arms from behind set me down, went forward with his key. At that moment, while I was free and they were all concentrating on the door, I got up, and, at a fast walk, started down the floor for the stairway and my cell.

When I was halfway down the floor to the stairs, the nervous concentrated-on-the-door guards looked back, saw that I was gone. One spied me forty feet away, walking for the stairs, called out: "There he goes!"

I walked along, at the same speed. I heard the guards break into a run, heard them getting closer and closer. As they grabbed hold of me, I relaxed, slumped to the floor.

One of the guards, whose last name was Berkowsky, then motioned the other guards back. "Let me handle him... Let me handle him. I can make him walk."

He took my right arm, put it behind my back, began twisting and pulled it upward in sharp little jerks. "O.K., now," he said with each upward jerk, "Walk. Get up and walk."

I remained motionless. He pulled up on my arm, my weight hung on it——

Booooo Boooooooo... Loud boos came from the tier-walks

above us. Booooo... then came loud catcalls. I looked up. It was four-thirty, the men were coming in from work. They stood at the railings of the upper tiers.

"What's the matter down there, can't you handle him? What's the matter with you four big guys—can't you handle that little ole boy? What are you trying to do, break his arm?" More prisoners were coming onto the tier-walk to boo.

I said to Mr. Berkosky: Go ahead, break it if you want... Go ahead." Mr. Berkosky continued to twist and pull up.

The Doctor, Mr. Sturgell, watched for a moment more, then shouted: "Don't! You'd better stop, you'll break it."

Mr. Berkosky let go of my arm. The other guards rushed forward to pick me up. The men up on the tier walks above continued to boo and shout.

The guards took me quickly out of the cell house through the now open door. They carried me down a short corridor, then up a flight of stairs. At the top of the stairs I found I was in the hospital—again being put into an observation cell. I was placed on the floor. A guard attendant came in, said to me: "Strip, we'll give you a pair of pyjamas." The carrying guards began to leave.

As soon as I saw they were going to leave me alone, I got up. They went out, locked the door behind them.

September-November, 1941.

The next day Doc Sturgell and the hospital guards either avoided me or were overly courteous. It appeared they were lying low, hoping I would not bring charges against them for a possible arm injury.

My clothes were returned, the cell door left open. I was told not to go out of the building. I didn't feel obliged to be my own jailer, so whenever I felt like it I went into the yard to play ball and talk to the other prisoners. About the fourth day a guard discovered that I had gone to the library to read. He "rang" the front office. Shortly I was back in the cell, the door locked.

In the days that followed, Doc Sturgell would come to my cell once a day, ask: "How are you, Naeve?" They would put in food, give me books and old magazines. To get anything else, I found I would have to beg, so I didn't ask for anything.

A few days passed. They didn't care, apparently, whether I had a bath or not. Finally I decided to make my own. I was filthy.

I stripped, filled the cell's small washbowl with water, splashed the water onto me with one hand, rubbed with the other. When the bowl became empty, I refilled it, repeated the process. The floor was flooded with water.

As I was drying myself, feeling much cleaner, I heard a key in the door. A guard shouted in: "What's this water doing out in the corridor?"

"I've just taken a bath." I explained I hadn't been given a bath in nine sweaty hot September days. If you were as dirty as I am, you'd take a bath out of the bowl, too." The guard left, returned, told me they were putting me on the schedule for a shower every two days....

... ...

November, 1941-February, 1942

...I was moved back to close-custody house, given a cell on the first floor. The authorities informed me they would leave my cell door open if I did as told—they were giving me a last chance. I told them I would not obey their orders, and they again locked me up.

The first afternoon I spent most of my time walking up and down. There was no outside window, only bars at one end. The space beside the bunk was about big enough to lie down in. I walked up and down in it. In the evening the other prisoners came to the front of the cell, told me: "You'll go nuts in there. Hell, you'll never be able to finish your seven months that way."

The first evening I lay on my bunk thinking: What a strange thing to be sitting in a cell objecting to a war that hadn't even started! November, 1941—I wondered, when would the war begin?

The first, the second day—At meal-times a tray of food was slid under the locked cell gate. I washed the ink off Life magazine paper, looked into my small cell mirror, did self-portraits for practice.

My days were well-filled, going quickly. Occasionally other prisoners stopped by. From them I learned the latest prison news. The divinity students' time had expired—Warden Gerlach was on a trip to Washington—"The menu for tomorrow I hear is...."

But one thing more than anything else began to occupy my time. The cell house wasn't heated in the daytime. I had to walk up and down to keep warm. I put my jacket on, and began —Four up, four back, four up, four back—I was beginning to get the steps just the right length. Then I discovered that by doing one sideways at one end I could go rhythmically in a circle. Four up—one across—four back—and repeat. This was the best. After two days I got so I could walk up and down nearly without looking.

On the third morning a guard came down and announced that the gate would be opened each morning so I could go over to the mess hall. If I didn't go over, I wouldn't get breakfast. I felt they were only baiting me, trying to get me back into the regimentation. I never went.

A week, ten days passed. I refused to do anything for the authorities, stayed in my cell. The prisoners who had ridiculed my bucking the regimentation slowed up, took me more seriously.

The breakfast baiting went on for about three weeks, then one morning a short fat officer named Fenton approached the front of my cell. "Ya know, Naeve, I could give you breakfast if you would just be a good boy. Three meals are better'n two. What do you say?"

I had been extremely agitated by the daily baiting. I hesitated to speak, growled inside, then answered: "I don't care, Mr Fenton, if you don't bring over any meals at all."

Mr Fenton paused, as if about to say something, then left. Soon I heard him phoning the "front office." "Ya know," he said in a slow casual drawl, "I was just talking to this fellow Naeve, just kidding him about the meals. I mentioned the fact we could give him breakfast, and he answers he don't care if we don't bring over any food at all." There was a silence; he was listening to the other end of the line. "O.K.," he concluded, "O.K." and hung up.

The next morning and the mornings after, I received breakfast.

It appeared the needling by officers was over, that for the rest of my time I'd be left pretty much alone... One evening I showed a friendly officer called Holmes some of my landscapes, including an off-hand sketch of Warden Gerlach. The next day my cell was 'shaken down' and literally every piece of drawing material was taken out. The order was, I was not to have pencil or paper in my cell. When I wanted to write a letter, I had to ask a guard for paper and pencil; when the letter was finished, the guard asked me to give everything back.

With no materials to draw with, my disgust reached a new low. Prisoners had offered to slip me pencils and paper, but I no longer wanted to draw or paint. I was weary of argument. Things that were taken from me before didn't seem to matter too much. But I had pulled into a cell, the last place to go, and still they refused to leave me alone. Somehow at this point my loathing for the prison and the way it was run enveloped me.

DECEMBER . . . .

As snow fell and the wind blew outside, the cell house became very cold. In the daytime I had to put on my coat and walk up and down, or stay in bed. I would walk up and down till I got tired, then crawl into bed. When I got tired of lying down, I'd walk some more.

December 7... A prisoner came rushing down to my cell: "Did you hear the news? They've bombed Pearl Harbor. It just came over the radio." Shortly Gene Garst, whom I'd met in quarantine, came to tell me the same thing. We looked silently at each other, just thought: It's finally begun.

... ...

In January, in the daytime I had to put on all my clothes and get into bed, or walk briskly up and down to keep warm. It didn't make much sense. There were cell houses that had heat all day. I asked Captain Thieman through a note for a change to another cell house. The request was ignored.

"My" cell was on the busiest corner of the cell house. I was put there, possibly, so the other prisoners might razz me and con me—"Ya can't beat the system." This did occur at first. But when the authorities baited me with the meals, wouldn't let me have pencil and paper to draw with, refused to move me to a heated cell house, all this changed. By January the men were still kidding, but differently. "That's the way, kid," they would say, "it's good to see somebody make a chump out of 'em. Just stick to guns. By the way, if there's anything you need, just tell me."

The men smuggled me food from the officers' mess—officers' eggs, officers' cheese. They slipped me pastry, candy. On several occasions a guard smelled the odor of strong cheese and shook the cell down. A built-in shelf under the table-top held the cheese. The perplexed guard sniffed, hunted. The hidden shelf and the cheese were never found.

One guard (an antique) was going into reverse. "They ought to allow you to paint. Maybe I can bring materials in to you" He offered to smuggle a set of water colors into the prison!

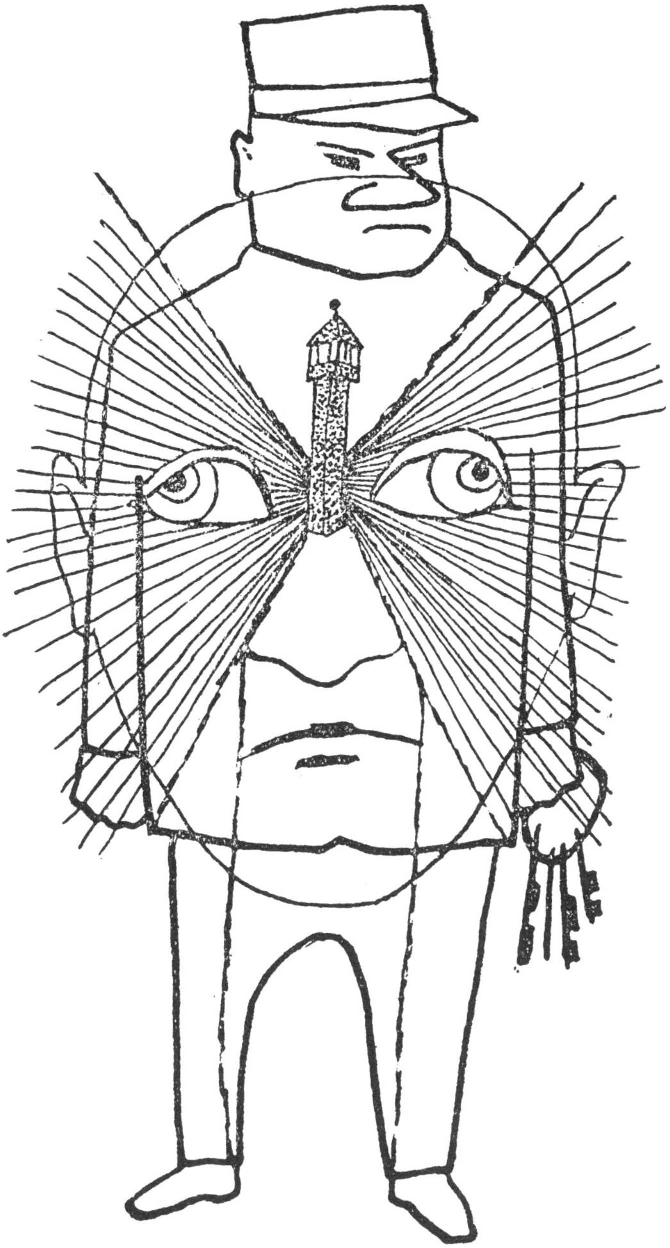

THE SHIP THAT NEVER HIT PORT

JAMES PECK

It was the morning of November 26, 1942.
When the heavy door of the courthouse elevator closed and the car moved slowly downward I felt that I was really on my way to jail. I had been pushed out of the federal courtroom by two hefty attendants while trying to deliver my anti-war spiel. A man should have his final say in court, I argued, but the judge would not listen. The two hefties grabbed my elbows. It had taken a little less than three minutes to sentence me to three years in federal prison.

In the receiving room we stripped and were told: "Spread your cheeks." Later I heard of a young religious CO who had come straight to jail from a sheltered home. When ordered to spread his cheeks, he put two fingers in his mouth and stretched.

After being thoroughly searched we got into prison clothes, regular work clothing except that the dungarees were light blue instead of dark. Next we went to the record office to fill out long questionnaires about our past history. One of the clerks was an inmate who must have been in for something like stock fraud, for it was easy to imagine him greeting fur-clad women in the uptown office of a leading brokerage firm. It is always this type who got the white collar jobs in jail.

Because it was a federal jail, West Street held few murderers. The only killers were men convicted of some federal offense in addition. A famous inmate was Louis Lepke, then sought by New York State authorities for the chair at Sing Sing. In West Street he was well liked because he was friendly with other inmates and told nothing to the authorities.

That is what counts in jail. What a man was sentenced for is almost immaterial. Unless an inmate talks about his case you do not question him.

Next to Lepke's cell at one time was a young CO from Iowa, Lowell Naeve, who later became an important figure at Danbury. He tried to explain to Lepke what a CO was but the gangster had trouble understanding.

"You mean they put you in here for not killing?" Lepke finally exclaimed—and he laughed and laughed.

Two other prominent inmates were George Browne and Willie Bioff, racketeering officials of the International Alliance of Moving Picture Operators and Theatrical Stage Employees. Both went out "to court" daily although their case was not being tried at the time. Rumor was that they saw their wives and had drinks in a private room at the courthouse. Anyway, both turned state's witness.

Days in West Street were not brightened by the building itself, a former warehouse and garage owned by Al Smith. Hardly any daylight got past the unwashed windows. The electric bulbs were high and dim, which made reading tough on the eyes. Coming into this semi-darkness after exercise on the fenced-in roof, we always squinted. The outside air, tho none too pure in New York, used to hit us like a shot of cold water after the foul air of the crowded cells.

The day began at 6 a. m. when, at the sound of the whistle, every man jumped from his bunk and stood by the bars for the first count. If we crawled back in our bunks for a few minutes there would probably be a recount and we would have to stand again.

There was counting all day long because of faulty reckoning of the turnover.

Breakfast was over by 7, leaving 14 hours before the lights would go out. In West Street there were not enough jobs for all the inmates and those who could not work had to stay in their cells. I was one of them. After breakfast I would read a book from the prison library, until my eyes tired at about 9 a. m. Then I would walk up and down the few paces within the cell block, and perhaps talk a bit with some of the other men. Next I would have a game of chess So it went throughout the day.

We all looked forward to our hour on the roof in the afternoon. Spirits were higher, too, in the evening, as one more day ended. The best bull sessions were held after the lights went out, and the invariable subject was women. In my cell block the participants were two Bundists, a man who had done time in Dannemora, toughest prison of New York state; and a kid who had been picked up after losing his draft card. We all got along well.

A favorite topic of the bull sessions was the the doings of Joe the Grinder—the guy who makes time with your girl while you do time.

"Well, Joe must be starting his rounds now," someone would say as the lights went out.

"Not so loud, or you'll have Mike blowing his top again".

Mike was doing tough time. Every night he would pace his cell and moan. A married man, he was in love with another girl and the officials would not let her visit or write him.

"How would you like to turn in with Lana Turner, tonight?" asked the kid.

"You wouldn't know what to do with her, for chrissake."
Everybody laughed-

"What's the hottest woman you ever had?"

"A Mexican in L. A." said the man from Dannemora, who was pacing and smoking. "Hell, it's been so long since I had a piece of ass I forget what it feels like."

"You won't forget how to do it when you get out, don't worry," put in one of the Germans.

"No, I ain't worrying and what's the hottest one you ever had?"

"Me, I'm a married man."

Everybody guffawed again.

"Don't tell me you wouldn't take any on the side. If a slick chick walked in this cell and put her arms around you?"

But there wasn't any slick chick, just the gang of us. People on the outside sometimes shiver at the thought of "associating with common criminals." In jail I found that the inmates are no different from any group of men picked at random on the outside. There is the same percentage of regular guys, the same percentage of phonies.

Movies were keenly anticipated. Each film was that much time spent on the outside. War pictures, serious films, and sticky romances were least popular; comedies and musicals were the favorites. Any reference to prisons, cops, or the law got a big laugh.

But with the end of the picture the men's troubles hit them harder. You could see it in their faces as the hacks ordered them back to their cells, like the housewife trudging back from the theatre to her slum dwelling. Somebody would kid about the leading woman, asking, "How would you like to find her in your bunk tonight?" There wouldn't be many laughs, yet the following day the men would already be asking what film was scheduled for the next week.

Sundays were especially dismal. Sitting in our semi-dark cells we could overhear the religious services, with hymn-singing that reminded me of a Bowery mission. And somehow there is a deadness about Sunday which you can feel even in mid-ocean.

We got a break Sunday nights, however, when the inmates staged a show. The MC was a fairy who made the rounds of the cell blocks scouting talent. One act was a game in which blindfolded inmates tried to pin a tail on a cardboard donkey. Grown men got a kick out of this childhood pastime.

In another act, a fairy with peroxided hair sang "Somebody else has taken my place." He sang like a strip teaser from burlesque. The more the audience yelled and catcalled, the more sexy his gestures became. After an encore he left the stage, glowing over his success, and was well goosed by the audience. The Negroes put on the best acts—plenty of rhythm and life for singing, dancing and comedy.

Visits were the biggest breaks for the men who had them. For several days these fellows would count on the meeting, and afterward they would keep thinking about it. The drawback is that after a visit a man usually does tougher time. The encounter is like a teaser—the outside is dangled before you for an hour and then yanked away. That is why some men don't want any visits.

At West Street the visiting room was a madhouse. The inmates were separated from their guests by a glass partition and talked with phones. One man would be shouting frantically what his lawyer should be told. Another would be bawling out his wife. A couple in love would simply stare at each other, minute after minute. A fat woman would be shushing her yowling kids, and another woman would be crying. Always the inmates and visitors were tense, trying to cram as much as possible into the brief period. Every now and then one of the supervising guards would come up to announce that somebody's time was up.

Nobody knew in advance when he would be transferred from West Street to the prison where he would do his time, nor was there any way of learning what prison it would be. The outgoing prisoner would simply be called to the receiving room one morning, be given his clothes, and be taken to a car by a couple of marshals.

That was how it happened with me. After 10 days in the detention house any change was welcome.

We were bound for Danbury. On the way I got my first dose of CO-baiting, though it was mild enough. In West Street the general comment on COs was that they were foolish to stick their necks out. There was no sneering.

... ...

When you are put in solitary the hacks remove your shoe laces and belt to guard against suicide. Locked in a 5x8 cell 24 hours a day without anything to read, a man has too much time to think. And with too much time to think a man starts wondering what's the use of it all.

The routine is the same: One, two, three, four steps—the iron door. Turn around. One, two, three, four steps—the wall. Turn around. One, two, three. four steps—the iron door. No sound except the clop, clop of your laceless shoes.

The solitary cells, known in Danbury as the bing, are on the top floor of the maximum custody cell block. Each cell has a massive iron door with a 3- by 6- inch peephole like the speakeasies had. Through this hole comes the only daylight, and through it the screw looks when he makes the count or an occasional inspection. Each cell has an electric bulb, almost useless without reading matter.

You have to pace the cell because walking is the only thing you can do and because you must get tired enough to sleep at night.

When I was in the hole this first time the only places to sit were the concrete floor and the porcelain toilet bowl, both of them cold. Blankets were brought at night and removed in the morning. About a year later a man got seriously ill from lying on the concrete and beds were then installed.

You think until your head aches and then you fall into a daze. After a while you start thinking again. You think about the prison setup, which Federal Prisons Director James V. Bennett calls "the most authoritarian in the world." You think about the screws who keep you locked in like an animal because they get orders from their superiors who get orders from higher officers who get orders from Washington.

Human consideration is not allowed at any point. And this whole prison machinery is at the service of the upperdogs to suppress the underdogs and mark as criminal those who try to get rich without using a respectable front.

You get to feeling pretty bitter about the system. You imagine yourself breaking into Bennett's lush office in Washington and telling him this is no way for a civilized country to act.

Then you get tired of thinking and lapse into a daze again.

But before long you find yourself thinking some more—you can't help it. You relive incidents and episodes; what you said, what the other person said, what you answered. Then you go over the entire scene again, but this time you think of what you should have said and what the other person would have answered. Then you mull over the names of place you have been, names of streets, names of night joints, names of girls.

I liked the noise of the ventilation system because it reminded me of a ship's engines. Often I would close my eyes and imagine myself aboard ship again. I would think of a warm, starry night in the Caribbean with the sea calm and the land-smelling breezes blowing from the islands. Then I would open my eyes and remember that it was only mid-morning.

Only breaks in the day were the meals, brought from the messhall in the regular tin trays. At that time you had to eat on either the toilet bowl or the floor, since there were no bunks. One inmate went on a hunger strike in protest. A guard brought the doctor, who asked him, "Why don't you just pretend it's a picnic?" The iron door was slammed with that advice but a few days later the striker was released from solitary.

I have seen men blow their tops in the hole. They start yelling and pounding on the iron door. One fellow cut loose about an hour before he was due to come out. He thought that the time for his release had passed and that he had been forgotten. Because of the rumpus he was kept in the hole three days longer.

Another man was put in the hole after a fight in the kitchen. The authorities did not know who started the fight but locked this man up just in case. After a few days he began screaming for the warden, the captain, the priest and his mother. He shouted that he would tell the whole story if they would only let him out. The captain came up, got the story and locked the door again.

The prisoner yelled even louder when the captain left but he finally got tired.

Solitary confinement is called isolation. In Danbury the maximum is 10 days, after which the prisoner is transferred to a modified form of solitary called segregation. The two advantages of segregation are that reading matter is permitted and the iron door is left open, letting light through the barred gate to the cell.

Another gain is that smoking is allowed in segregation. Regular guys in segregation used to pack the light-switch box with tobacco and matches. If the cell were used next by a man in isolation, he could have tobacco. Sometimes the screws got the idea of shaking down these cells but they did not do it often.

Cigarets are occasionally sneaked in with meals, hidden between slices of bread. An inmate caught doing this would be thrown in the hole himself. Before it became general policy to close the iron doors it was easier for men in isolation to get smokes. Friends would throw cigarets from the gate to the catwalk which runs in front of the solitary cells. The prisoner would take off his monkeysuit (coveralls) and throw one end through his gate bars to the catwalk. If it was a good shot the package would be covered. Then the prisoner would pull in the monkeysuit very slowly so the cigarets would not slip from under. It was like landing a fighting fish.

A smoke in solitary is as good as a drink in the desert. But you must keep a careful lookout for the screw and flush your butt down the toilet. If a screw smelled smoke or saw any butts, there would be a shakedown followed by tighter regulations.

Sometimes the man throwing cigarets down the catwalk makes a bad shot and the package lands before an empty cell, hopelessly beyond reach. It remains there until a screw picks it up. One screw was mean enough to open the package and light up before a prisoner in solitary. Another fellow and I were caught once when we were throwing cigarets. We were put in solitary for three days with seven more days in segregation.

A gang of us were in solitary when the iron doors were

left open. An inmate on the outside tossed a full pack of cigarets down the catwalk and missed. I was closest—only four cells away (about 20 feet) All of us were craving a smoke and were determined not to let the screw get this package.

We made a long rope by ripping up our BVDs and tying the strips together. I took off one of my shoes and secured it to the end of the rope. Then I coiled the rope, reached out through my gate bars and hurled the shoe down the catwalk to fall just beyond the cigarets. This was guesswork, since I could not see the package.

I pulled in the rope very gently, but no luck. I cast the line again. No cigarets. This went on for about an hour. I was in a sweat. If a screw appeared we would lose the tobacco, there would be a crackdown on smoking and my time in solitary would be extended.

Apparently some of my throws were bringing the package a few inches closer for at last it came into view before my cell. The other fellows cheered as I ripped the rope into small pieces and flushed it down the toilet. It was easy to pass the smokes around via the catwalk since we were in adjacent cells.

When the iron doors were open a man in solitary could talk to, or rather shout to, the other prisoners. This was a big help in killing time. But when the authorities decided to close the doors the only conversation was with men in adjacent cells by yelling through the ventilator. If the cells next door were empty you could not talk at all.

My first time in solitary I had nobody to talk to for a week. Three of us had been locked up for striking against a longer work week, but we were not put in adjoining cells. Although the prison authorities issue high-sounding statements about work being a privilege, it is compulsory. Men refusing to work get severe penalties.

Punishment is meted out by a 3-man board called the Adjustment Council, which consists of the associate warden, one of the prison doctors and one of the parole officers. *All the forms of a fair trial are carefully observed but no inmate is ever acquitted.*

The accused man always gets so many days of isolation, segregation or restriction (being locked in a solitary cell except when working or eating).

Actions which in the outside world would be called common sense are often counted as offenses in prison. One toothless prisoner was locked up because he could not chew liver and left it on his tray. Frequently the liver was so tough that men with perfect teeth could not handle it.

Nine of us were once put in solitary for leaving sour sweet potatoes on our trays. We were all at the same table so the authorities probably thought it was an agitators' plot. Called into the Adjustment Council together, each of us had his say.

I told the board I could bring in other inmates who would testify that the spuds were sour and they had eaten them only to keep out of trouble. This offer was not taken up.

Another prisoner, a New England fisherman, made a real fight. This man had weather-toughened skin and close-cropped, graying hair. Among the inmates his attitude was good-humored cynicism, and he made no effort to hide from the officials his contempt for the prison setup. No matter how often he was put in the hole, the officials could not break him.

On this occasion the fisherman pulled from his pocket a sample potato which he had wrapped in his handkerchief and sneaked out of the messhall. He showed it to the doctor.

Dr. Sturgell smiled benignly.

"The potatoes were good. It is just your imagination."

"I suppose the rotten meat loaf was good too the time that 50 men puked after eating it."

"Yes, the meat loaf was good."

"I suppose it was just their imagination, too."

"That is correct. Haven't you ever heard of mass hypnosis?"

"You are a liar."

The fisherman was about to broaden his remarks when another prisoner cut in.

"Take it easy. You can't win in this setup. They'll only keep

"IT'S A GRUESOME JOB"    "BROTHER THERE AINT NO GRAFT IN THIS JAIL"

WAITING FOR THE PENSION 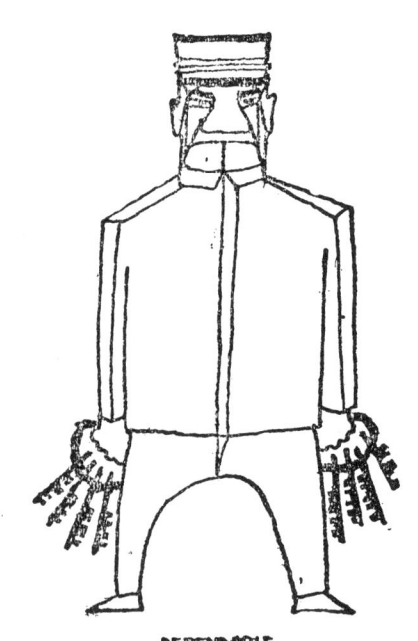   DEPENDABLE

"I'D QUIT IF IT WASN'T FOR MY WIFE"   "GOOD PAY"

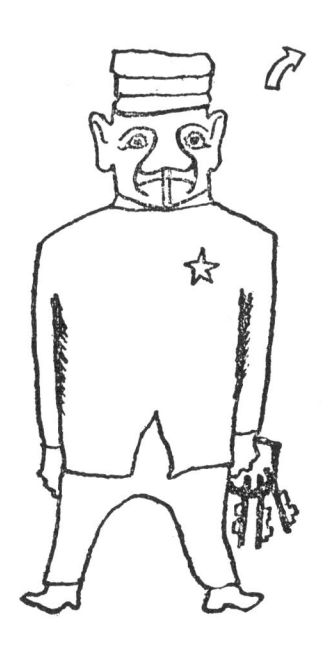

HOW DID I BECOME A PRISON HACK? WELL, I WOULDN'T CALL IT THAT, CUSTODIAL OFFICER WOULD BE MORE APPROPRIATE, THAT'S OUR RATING IN THE BLUE BOOK.
....IN 1939 I WAS JUST OUT OF HIGH SCHOOL. LIKE MOST OTHER KIDS I DIDN'T KNOW WHAT I WANTED TO DO, EXCEPT I RECOGNISED I WAS A LITTLE DIFFERNT. I DIDN'T WANT ANY OLD JOB. I WANTED SOMETHING WHERE I COULD DO SOME GOOD.
    AFTER 4 YEARS IN COLLEGE I SOMEHOW DECIDED TO GET INTO SOCIAL WORK... I WANTED A GOVERNMENT JOB. WHEN I LOOKED INTO THIS POSSIBILITY I FOUND THAT PRISON WORK WAS A FIELD THAT WAS WIDE OPEN.
    I WAS PRETTY IDEALISTIC AT FIRST, DIDN'T WANT TO BE A KEY MAN. I WANTED TO SUPERVISE RECREATION, YOU KNOW UMPIRE BASE BALL GAMES, REFEREE BOXING MATCHES AND THE LIKE. BUT AFTER I GOT ON THE JOB (I WAS MARRIED BY THIS TIME) I FOUND THE BUREAU OF PRISONS WAS'NT TOO IN--TERESTED IN RECREATION FOR PRISONERS. AND- -WELL - BUT! IV'E STILL GOT MY IDEALS.

PRISON GUARDS BY *Lowell Naeve*

you in the hole longer."

The last witness was a Chinese whose policy was not to speak English when dealing with the authorities. He read a lot and was an expert pinochle and checker player, but with the front office it was "No savvy."

"And what have you got to say?" asked the associate warden.

"Me taste, potato sour, no eat."

Even the associate warden was forced to laugh.

In accordance with the traditions of the court we were all found guilty and penalized. The fisherman was told to remain when we left but luckily his penalty was no more than ours: 12 days restrictions. The solitary cell block was the noisiest part of the prison during our stay. Since the iron doors are open for men in restrictions, we could conduct endless bull sessions and a great deal of singing. Our improvised songs were "It's a yam session" and "Oh no, the spuds were not sour, it's imagination."

Poor grub is the number one grievance in prison. Unpopular dishes are always razzed. One Sunday evening the main dish was stale bread soaked in a yellowish sauce made of flour and faintly flavored with cheese. Labeled cheese fondue, it was the butt of jokes for days and never was served again.

Another one-meal flop bore the title of *pasta y fasule*. It was the two suppertime steadies, beans and macaroni, mixed together.

For a long period the breakfast fruit was prunes one morning, raisins the next, then prunes again. At last the menu showed a change to "mixed fruit". It was prunes and raisins.

When kidding did not remove an unpopular dish, some of the men would propose that we all refuse to eat it. Usually the boycott idea did not get past the discussion stage. But one time about a year after the sour sweet potato episode, a group of us decided to act.

Our grievance was scrapple, a doughy mass of cornmeal, fat, and other remnants, including a few hairs. The men were beefing in the yard after a scrapple supper.

"Next time they put out that God damn scrapple, everybody should refuse to eat it," one inmate remarked.

The idea happened to catch on and throughout the prison a boycott campaign got under way. In cell houses and dormitories both CO's and other inmates were busily promoting. The few stools who said, "It's just those damn COs" were laughed down by the non-COs.

One of the men coined a slogan: "Scrap the Scrapple." When scrapple next appeared on the menu the slogan was shouted openly all over the yard. At supper that night all but about 30 of the 600 inmates passed up the scrapple.

We did not see it again for eight months. Probably assuming that all had been forgotten the authorities tried scrapple again. The response was the same and the dish never came back. Somewhat like an employer who has lost a strike, the warden explained to one inmate that the boycott had nothing to do with the exit of scrapple—he had intended for some time to remove it.

The success of the scrapple boycott encouraged us to use the same tactic against another objectional dish, macaroni mixed with meatless pieces of bone. Apparently the warden had also intended to get rid of this mess.

...The worst period is the first couple of months in prison. Later a man gets more used to doing without a woman.

I missed the drinks even more than the women and a number of guys agreed with me. When you get the blues on the outside you can always kill them with a couple of drinks. But in jail you just have to wait until the blues wear off and that may take a long while.

As a substitute some of the men took nutmeg or ginger which were sneaked out of the kitchen. Mixed with water, either one will set you up. I tried nutmeg at Danbury for the first time. Because it does not dissolve, the drink is like sawdust but within a couple of hours you feel lighter than air. It is strange to have a nutmeg jag in prison and to laugh at the ridiculous screws with their keys and whistles. One little Negro, who had a stiff bit ahead of him after Danbury, managed to keep high most of the time. He was always laughing.

So much nutmeg and ginger disappeared from the kitchen that the authorities put them under lock and key. That made them highly valued connections. The kitchen is the main center of the connections trade. Men working there smuggle out eggs, meat, pies, apples and other food at the risk of being put in the hole. Some give the connections to their friends. Others sell them, and these prisoners are called merchants.

No money is passed, of course. The merchants use a barter system. For example, an inmate will pay for kitchen connections with cigarets, cigars or candy bought in the commissary. Or he may arrange for a return connection. If he worked in the clothing room, he could settle his debt by providing well fitting and neatly pressed clothing every week, or even a new coat or a new pair of shoes. An inmate who appeared in the yard with carefully ironed dungarees or new shoes would be greated with: "Connection man!"

Nutmeg and ginger are not wholly satisfactory substitutes for alcohol. Occasionally a resourceful prisoner would build a crude still, but no inmate was able to produce liquor in helpful quantities before the operation was discovered by the screws. At Christmas it was usually possible to get a drink or two, the rumor being that one lieutenant and a couple of screws would sell whiskey at $25 a bottle.

"It's a privilege to be in an institution like Danbury," the warden used to tell the inmates assembled for Saturday night movies.

Visitors used to admire the lawn and flowerbeds in the yard. The warden would explain that Danbury was not a prison at all but a correctional institution where men were "rehabilitated."

If the visitors were important the inmates got a special lunch, the kind usually served on Sundays. There would be a pork chop or another meat dish and dessert. Whenever a good lunch was served in midweek the word would pass, "There must be some bigshot visitors today." And there always were.

The biggest shot during my term was Attorney General Francis Biddle, who was accompanied by Federal Prisons Director Bennett, the warden and a couple of state troopers. For several days the inmates had been kept busy primping up the joint. Every brass doorknob was polished and even the unoccupied solitary cells were mopped and swept.

Biddle played the role of a democrat and talked with various groups of prisoners. When he approached several of us who were guinea pigs in a yellow jaundice experiment we delivered a blast against the labor draft bill then up in Congress.

"As a matter of fact I agree with the administration's support of the bill," was his comment. Then he asked the warden, "Are all the men in this group opposed to the bill?"

"Well, some are and some are not." the warden replied, characteristically.

Of course everyone in the jaundice experiment, including the non-CO's, was against the bill. While this discussion took place Prisons Director Bennett was nervously maueuvering his body to block Biddle's view of an empty cell which had been overlooked in the cleanup.

Biddle paused before a man reading a newspaper and asked him why he was in prison. The inmate, an Italian CO, barely looked up.

"Because I refuse to kill my mother," he replied and kept on reading.

The only visible result of Biddle's inspection was that shortly afterward the hacks resumed wearing their old caps with badges in front. A year or so before the caps had been replaced by black felt hats with wide brims, well suited to ministers of some obscure sect but not in character for the Danbury screws. The inmates had given these hats the razzberry and the screws themselves were not very happy about them.

The sudden disappearance of the hats was generally attributed to Biddle's disapproval.

"What happened to the hats?" one inmate asked.

"They are all at the cleaners," answered a screw who had a sense of humor.

A few weeks later the inmate remarked, "They're taking a hell of a long time to clean those hats."

The screw laughed.

Visitors never see the solitary cells unless they happen to be prison officials or penology students. After a tour conducted by the smiling warden, most sightseers conclude that Danbury is the Utopia of the prison system. The deception is natural. The prison does not resemble the traditional institution — dark, dingy and barred, surrounded by towering walls patrolled by guards. Danbury is a light-colored, modern, 2-story structure built around a large compound, with no outer wall and no bars outside the windows

The cell houses and dormitories are named for the New England States and their capitals, like the buildings of a swank private school. Instead of West Wing 3 or Cell Block 9 it is New Hampshire House, Providence House and so on. While I was there the authorities erected a fancy white highway sign which possibly led some motorists to assume that the jail was a renovated inn with a rich historic background.

"Behind this phoney facade is the most completely fascist setup you can imagine," I told one religious visitor who had been converted by the warden.

The core of fascist machinery is the disciplinary system, based on the theory that the inmate is always wrong. It is against regulations for screws to lay hands on inmates. One prisoner who started to argue when a guard manhandled him at the movies was written up (reported) and given a week in restrictions. We learned later that the screw was told by the front office that he was in the wrong, but it was the inmate who got punished.

Another screw chose as his victim an Italian kid who was in the hole. This youngster, who had seen too many gangster movies, liked to talk tough and had got into an argument with the screw. Inmates who were mopping the house a few days after the argument told us what had happened. The guard came up, carefully removed his watch and then unlocked the cell door. As soon as he stepped inside he started swinging. The boy fell back on his bunk but the screw kept hammering him. Blood flowed onto the mattress. Finally exhausted, the guard left.

When I heard of this beating I wrote a letter of protest to Prisons Director Bennett in Washington. A group of the Italian's friends drew up a petition. I showed my letter to the screw before sending it. He paled—for he had been in similar trouble at another prison—and I thought he was going to take a swing at me. But he decided to be smarter.

The authorities accused the kid of hitting the screw first and removed half of his goodtime. The screw was transferred to a late night shift, where none of the inmates saw him, and the bloody mattress was taken away and burned.

Then the screw tried to settle his score with me. He told some of the inmates that the kid would not have lost his goodtime if I had not written to Washington. When the young Italian heard this story he got mad and said he didn't want any God damn CO mixing up in his business. But his friends, who knew where I stood, told him never to believe a screw.

I was so griped by the framing of the boy that I went up front at noon to protest to the warden. The guard at the front gate said he was not in. I said I would wait. I was still waiting when the afternoon work whistle blew. A few minutes later I was called in but instead of meeting the warden I found the adjustment council in session. The council promptly sentenced me to three weeks' restrictions for "failure to report for work." I was put in a cell near the Italian kid and we got to know each other quite well.

The authorities were greatly annoyed by the strategy of one absolutist CO. He would not obey any order from any prison official.

If locked in a cell, he would yell as loud as he could for hours. Finally he was put in the hospital where he continued his policy of non-obedience.

We never managed to find out which prison official was responsible for moving a healthy and hardboiled inmate, whose profession on the outside was strikebreaking, into the hospital. The fink was brought in only a few days before his scheduled release and on his second night in the hospital he went to work on the CO, leaving a bad gash over the young man's eye.

Immediately the other COs started sending protests to Washington, for every prisoner has the theoretical privilege of writing uncensored complaints to the federal prisons director. Shortly afterward the beaten man was quietly released from Danbury under a special arrangement.

Once when Bennett was making his annual visit I told him that the inmates' sealed complaints were being opened and held up by the warden. I expressed the view that tampering with the mail was not generally recognized as legal.

"Most anything is legal in institutions like this," Bennett remarked, and walked on.

Screws who go out of their way to find trivial violations for which they can write a man up are spoken of as pricks. One type is the thick-headed cop who is impressed with the power of his badge and gets sadistic enjoyment from making the inmates more miserable than they already are. In state prisons this kind of guard beats up prisoners, but in federal prisons—except for occasional outbursts of violence—the tough screw has to be satisfied with merely making trouble.

Another type of prick is the young college graduate who regards his job as a stepping stone to a career in penology. He thinks that by enforcing every regulation he will climb faster, but the only result of his diligence is that a lot of inmates get into unnecessary trouble.

Many of these career men became hacks during the last depression and just stayed on. Some were idealistic enough to hope that they could improve conditions. But they soon found themselves as completely regimented as the inmates. Any order from the front office, no matter how much it sickened them, had to be carried out. During my term more than one career man quit in disgust.

One young screw became meaner and meaner as his disillusionment grew. When he first came on the job he would actually intercede with the front office on behalf of inmates getting a raw deal. The prison authorities retaliated by giving him the most disagreeable assignments and denying him the promotion he deserved from experience and education. The screw worked out his frustration and bitterness on the inmates, becoming as unpopular with them as with the front office. But he could not quit because he had a family to support.

The better hacks are usually the older men whose sole interest is job security and retirement benefits. They do not make petty trouble. Some really believe in treating the inmates as humanly as possible but nearly all of them accept the Prisons Bureau attitude that prisoners are inferior to other human beings.

All the hatred from jailhouse bitterness is focused on the prick type of screw. The judge who sentenced you is far away, the warden is out in the front office, but the hack is hounding you day after day, week after week.

One young southerner was especially nasty. Whenever he was on duty in the maximum custody cell block we showed our contempt for him by a method not covered in the prison regulations. As he passed each cell, making the count, the man inside would flush his toilet bowl and hold the lever down. The roar and gurgle steadily rose to the scale of a mountain waterfall, with 60 toilets flushing at once and a few shouts of "Heil Hitler!" echoing above the din.

We also found a way to handle a careerist who annoyed us in the messhall by reprimanding men who left knives, forks or spoons a quarter-inch or so off the prescribed position, or put the soup bowl in the section of the tray designed for the tin cup.

The screw would either rearrange the utensils himself, like a kindergarten teacher, or make the inmate do so. He would also bawl out inmates when the second button on their shirts was unfastened Because of his stringy red moustache this screw was known as The Brush.

After some thought and discussion we launched a Crush-the-Brush drive, A group of us agreed to leave our utensils in complete disorder. At first the Brush painstakingly reprimanded each offender and showed him him exactly where to place knife, fork, spoon, cup and bowl. Finally exasperated, he called for the lieutenant. This officer hurried over to one of the disorderly tables' shook his finger at us and bellowed: "From now on you'll have to deal with me!" But we had less trouble with the Brush afterward.

The hacks of course hold all the aces in dealing with any prisoner because they can always write him up for inevitable punishment. Every infraction of the rules is noted in the prisoner's jacket, a folder which records all the details of the man's life before and during imprisonment. There are general reports written by the work detail screw, the cell block screw, or some other screw who may have overheard a conversation. Tales pumped from stoolpigeons are also included.

Any letter which interests the authorities goes into the jacket. The mail censor may make a photostatic copy of a prisoner's entire letter, or merely copy a passage. Or he may pass the letter on to the warden. Often an inmate called out by the warden or parole officer is confronted with something he wrote so long ago he had forgot all about it. It might be about his personal life or his political views—a fragment of thought that the prison authorities felt was dangerous and filed for later use.

When I came to Danbury we were not allowed to mention the prison or the inmates in our letters. A man put in solitary could not say so. Upon request the office would send correspondents a form notice saying that correspondence privileges had been temporarily removed because of a violation of prison rules.

Constant pressure by COs and especially a combined work and hunger strike against censorship by COs in Lewisburg resulted in liberalization of the rules. Forbidden periodicals were admitted, and we were even allowed to write about prison happenings provided the reports were accurate. Of course any such comments went into the jacket.

Incoming mail was closely watched. One correspondent who severely criticized the prison system was stricken from the inmate's list of approved correspondents.

...We decided on strike action. The first step was to canvass the CO population to see how many would go along. Of course we ran into all kinds of arguments and doubts, even though all but one of the nearly 100 COs were opposed to Jim Crow...

We got together Tuesday evening and counted 17 men pledged to strike. Later that night a young CO we had not even bothered to canvass said he would join making it 18. Our procedure was to boycott the messhall next morning and then refuse to work...

...Instead of being taken to one of the 13 solitary cells in the maximum custody cell block, we were led to a small recreation room, facing the yard, in another cell house called Upper Hartford The reason was plain when we entered the room and found all of the other 16 strikers present...

The officials had decided to convert the entire second floor into special solitary quarters for the strikers...

The solid steel doors had small windows through which we could look across the hall and see the man in the opposite cell if he were standing at his door. But the most valuable feature of the cell design was the three-quarter inch space between the bottom of the door and the concrete floor. These openings enabled us to conduct strike meetings and hold bull sessions by lying on the floor with our mouths at the slot. Since the concrete was cold, we used to spread our blankets for a lengthy meeting.

The slots also proved handy for passing around newspapers,

magazines and notes. Any business we wanted to keep secret had to be transacted by notes, for when we talked under the doors we never knew whether or not a hack was listening at the end of the hall.

On Thanksgiving Day, when we were allowed for the first time to eat together in the recreation room, we got a look at the daily record book kept by the screws supervising us. Through an oversight it had not been locked up.

On one page a snooping hack had written: "When I arrived a heated discussion was in progress underneath the doors and they were taking a vote on I don't know what."

Another page had an entry quoting one of us: "This grub isn't fit for a dog. Don't eat it."

But the most amusing notation was this: "I discovered an ingenious device which they used for passing periodicals from cell to cell and I seized it."

Until then we had referred to these gadgets as carriers but we promptly changed the name to ingenious devices. We had invented them the first day of the strike. Clipped around the radiator pipes, where the pipes entered the wall, were the metal discs found in every private home with plumbing. Since they were thin enough to pass under the doors, we pulled them loose and attached 8-foot lengths of string. At first we built our string from the loops on Bull Durham tobacco bags (called Stud in Danbury), distributed free by the prison. Later we got hold of an old mop which supplied us for the duration.

At the other end of the string we would tie the papers or notes to be passed. Then we would get on the floor and zip the metal gadget underneath the door, across the hall and into the cell opposite—or the cell on either side of the opposite one. The man in that cell would pull the string until the message came into his cell. By zigzagging the length of the hall we could reach every striker.

Sometimes we had to make several tries before getting the disc under the opposite door. To silence the noise of metal scraping against concrete we wrapped the discs in paper or cloth. Naturally we did not use the ingenious devices when we knew that hacks were around but occasionally we guessed wrong. During the strike we lost 4 discs from our stock of 36, hardly enough to qualify the hacks as super-snoops.

Once the prison psychiatrist was peering down our hall from the hospital door. He saw a folded paper moving slowly across the hall, apparently under its own power for at that distance the thin string was not discernible. The doctor unlocked the door and dashed down the hall but the paper had been jerked into a cell at the sound of the lock. Abruptly halting, the doctor stared at the bare floor and the solid cell doors with the kind of expression usually seen on his patients.

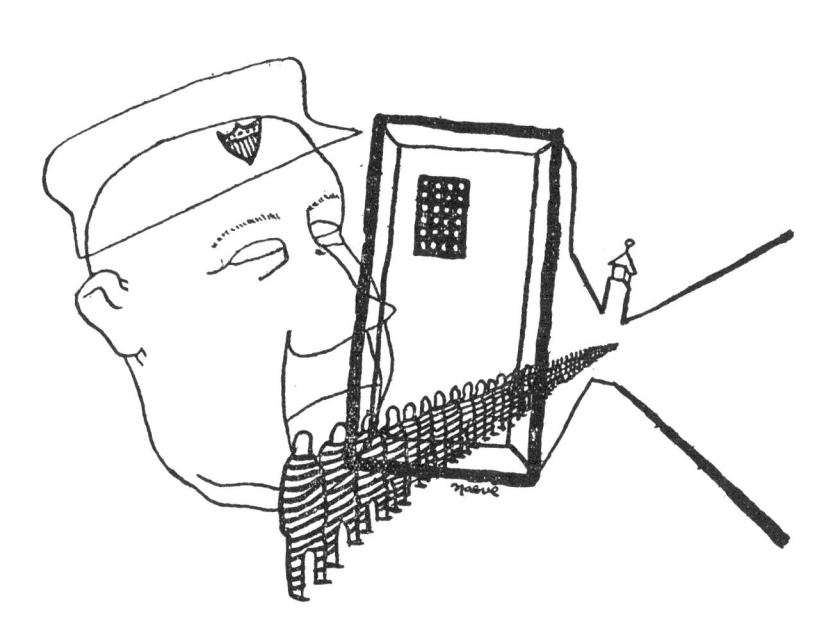

... ...

SECTION TWO

THE PRISON COMMUNITY

"THE DAY ITSELF DOES HARD TIME"

NOTES ON MY LIFE AMONG THE DEAD MEN IN DENIMS

CURTIS ZAHN

The *Catalina Highway* begins as one of those monotonous straight lines drawn across the fiery sands of Arizona desert near Tucson, then suddenly hairpins itself up into pines and pinnacles to an ultimate elevation of 12,000 feet. To the sightseer it offers numerous awful wonders; grotesque stone shapes which—according to the Pima County Highway Department—resemble ducks, dwarves and elephants. The motorist entertains the fool notion that were his car to leave the road on certain of the curves, it could plummet through space for twenty or thirty miles before striking land. The rocks—and they are everywhere in varying degrees of size or shape —appear ready to crash downward at the thrust of a chipmunk. The weather itself exhibits animosity toward the tourist, angering up blasts of 120 degrees which produce engine vapor lock in the draws while permitting ice to chill its clients in the higher regions. Cloudbursts and dramatic electrical displays are common, and snow is not otherwise, and all flora and fauna have been stunted, frustrated and worn weary by the Lord's mighty elements.

But, offsetting these discouragments to tourists who may have dared the trip without air-conditioning are numerous man-made comforts. A plasterer by trade whose avocation was forging checks built three stone drinking fountains which yield cool water. Both automobile and driver patronize these shrines which could be called functional monuments to the truism that crime doesn't pay. There exists a dramatic view spot where sweaty pilgrims may park their dusty new Buicks and gaze across fifty miles of sand, stone and cacti. A young man from Florida—who, for discretion's sake shall be called Mr 4937—got a broken leg from a dynamite accident here in 1944. Farther on, you get into the pines and it is cool. Wild turkeys and deer are to be seen, and here, once were camp fires built by shivering men who labored in snow. Often a 16 pound sledge missed its chisel and smashed stiff fingers. Often too, a chow truck bogged down and a hundred laborers waited a half hour longer than usual for cabbage, beans, black coffee, brown bread and saccherine-tinted starch pudding.

The vacationist is unlikely to note the innumerable small bridges over which he drives, for his eyes are already dedicated to the task of negotiating curves, and whatever kind of visual surplus remains is instantly captured by lush glens or sterile panoramas. Most of the arches were built by a group of Missionaries from the religious sect known as Jehovah's Witnesses, and who believed themselves ordained ministers. None of them had previous experience in masonry and a few of them worked at this employment on December 25, 1944. At one point the motorist is afforded a quick look at Tucson. Many of the laborers who built the road are said to have gazed wistfully, whenever possible, at this sight. For this glimpse—however distant—was for months and sometimes years their only contact with the outside world. Probably they experienced a kind of nostalgic, quiet well-being just to know that another civilization still existed, even though their very presence on the Catalina Highway indicated that they somehow had gotten out of step with society in general.

Eventually, the indefatigible motorist arrives at the summit where is located Mt. Lemon resort—long a mecca for people who find themselves forced to reside in Arizona the year round. But before arriving, he will have passed the exact point at which two draft evaders had been seized and handcuffed by officers of the law. Both had taken longer than ten minutes to answer the call of nature. And because no one should require longer than that maximum considering the diet of roughage offered to laborers here, they were shipped to the Reformatory at La Tuna, Texas. The vacationist will also have passed such historical shrines as the knoll where an ex-scholarship football player threw down his shovel and wept; where a young Minister quoted Scripture to seven Mexican border jumpers, two Negroes and a Navajo, who, it was rumored, would steal any motorcycle in Arizona for fifty dollars. Assuredly, none of this *Cataliana* was judged sufficiently documentary to warrant attention; no signs advertise these locations But it is generally remembered that the fifteen mile highway has the distinction of being hand-carved—that it was hewn almost entirely without machinery and took sixteen years and several hundred men.

But, if the *Catalina Highway* stole a portion of life from an awful lot of people, it also helped the populace by protecting it from these same men. During world war two, it kept undesirable citizens from joining the armed forces. It prevented 60 conscientious objectors from objecting too publically, shielded the U. S. citizenry from at least 200 Jehovah's Witnesses, 31 Japanese Americans, five Russian Molokans and seven Hopi Indians—all of them selective service cases. The highway also provided avocation for men who stole automobiles, forged checks, murdered, impersonated officers, impersonated women or jumped borders or transported individuals of the opposite sex across state lines.

Judging by today's wage minimums, the paying back of a debt to society was ridiculously easy for the criminal fortunate enough to gain admittance here. For, in charge of construction (though supervised by civilian engineers) was Federal Road Camp Number Ten—an experiment in incarceration that was called by Westbrook Pegler the "Tucson Country Club." The prisoner worked nine hours per day and six days per week. The overhead—the cost of maintanance per man—must have been startlingly low; the prison was almost self sufficient, having its own laundry, mending, farms, hogs, etc. The items that were imported often came from other Federal Institutions and, at the same time, Tucson Road Camp often swapped labor or furniture or produce with independent local producers. Too, the fact that a man who stole a nickel worked just as hard and sometimes as long as a man who stole a million dollars—plus the obvious statistic that an infinitely larger nickel-thieving group is apprehended than that of the million dollar species—suggests that, if anything, society is indebted to the prisoner.

2

In Arizona, the day itself does hard-time. From dawn until dark it sweats it out and finally sinks into bed weary and beaten and sunburned. Yet, on the following morning, the day is up miraculously early, smiling and fresh like a Saturday child, ready to try again. The landscape is neat, clean, sterile. The lizards do push-ups all day long. They sprawl full length in the sun's relentless glare upon scorched, glistening rocks and, with their pin-sized forearms, raise their scaly bodies up and down. Clear, searing days chastise any other creature that dares move in broad daylight. A fiery morning sun cooks the cold out of Joshua trees; thaws the cactus, gives hope to the piñon pines and junipers—then tortures them until twilight. The bleak wastes seem to smile at the plants and animals which sit stoicly upon them and dream of a better day or, more accurately dream of night. Only the lizards and the prisoners move, the former voluntarily, the latter involuntarily. The latter move because a large bureau in Washington says that they shall move. They move mountains in an assiduous endeavor to pay back their debt to society.

The prison guards are apathetic. They are trapped somewhere between Government orders, humanism and the economic situation. They suffer like the prisoners for they are assigned the task of making the prisoners ache their backs in the torrid heat, and they long since have been cleaned of the theories about punishment. In summer, the guards wear sun helmets and constantly mop their brows and glance hopefully at their watches. They see bronzed muscular bodies strain, and sweat; they seek escape by staring up at occasional passing warplanes that drone like hot eagles in the sky. They pause to watch an unearthed chipmunk or scorpion brought up on a shovel. They sit on hot rocks, only to leap up again, then sit down again somewhere else. They are one man against fifty, Gods or dictators for the duration of a sentence. They did not necessarily want to do this. Most men would have carefully been screened from such employment. But they did want a job, and this is a job.

Time is on the side of the prisoner. Each time the watch comes out, a few minutes of life have run out. A few minutes gone is a few minutes towards freedom for the inmate. There were left—even as I wrote this—only 344 days, seven hours and 22 minutes before *dressing out*. Dressing out is the hour by which every inmate measures time. It comes but once for every conviction. No event, including the coming of Christ, could sit alongside that occasion. It is hallowed and hushed and anguished. It is a time when the inmate sheds his prison skin for an hour and tries on a suit of clothes made perhaps in Alcatraz, shoes from Atlanta Reformatory, necktie by Sing-Sing, BVD's by Springfield. In a few weeks, theoretically speaking, it will have been tailored to fit, theoretically speaking. There will be ten dollars in the right rear pants pocket and the suit's occupant will clutch a bus ticket home. A prisoner might be heard to remark some night when the lights are out, "only two more Fourth of July's and one Thanksgiving until dressing out,". Or—and this hysterically—"only 17 more work days until dressing out." Like misers they count statistics, invent complicated little games; ("only fifteen more eggs until dressing out.") [There are exactly 52 eggs per year per man.]

But to the jailors time is an enemy. They are getting no younger and they do not like this job and are afraid to quit and seek employment elsewhere. They see the inmate walk leadenly into camp and leave on innocent wings. They cannot help jealousy over the sky rockets of sheer animation which must come at least once to every inmate here. They, alas, must stay behind year after year, imprisoned by life or by their own fear of insecurity. They must daily feel the guilt projected by whoever assumed the duty of making another suffer. For, who in prison has a guilty conscience? Guilt is, in this case, merely intellectual; the scale has been balanced by the time the New Fish has had his shots, and from then on he is as innocent as his captor. And the jailor is let know that the line between guilt and innocence is almost transparent. Every crime might be your crime.

The jailor fears that the prisoner might do well on the outside. Might live a normal, pleasant existance, or successfully steal thirty thousand and buy a ranch in Texas. Or legally earn thirty thousand. But the guard will stay on. While he does, he cannot earn or steal thirty thousand. Nor can he predict with confidence that on such and such a date—exactly three months, 24 days, and 5 hours and 4 minutes—he will leave prison.

The parts are switched then. Certain insecurities are healed for the duration of a sentence of a prisoner. No matter what he does, nothing can happen worse than this. He is now living the lowest common denominator and anything—most anything at all —will be a step up. Except death. That is the last unknown. But life and death, like guilt and innocence, are almost twins here. To have lived in prison is to have died in theory. The First-Timer, indeed, begins his sentence quite dead and gains life as he approaches the end. The jailor starts work alive and dies slowly, and there is no "after life"—no post prison world—on his horizon. He awakes to fear, old age, unemployment, death. The prisoner's daily birth brings another night accomplished, another numeral crossed off the calendar. Old age and unemployment present exciting opportunities as against the present.

3

We are an island. Encircled by sterile stony hills to the northwest and parched sandflats to the southeast, the grey-green barracks are bound to civilization only by the coils of road and a telephone wire. But it is self-sufficient. Heat and light are provided by generators which burn logs provided by the woodcutting crew. Water comes from the prison camp's own well. Tucson—a neonic city in the desert—is less than thirty miles away but you cannot hear it it, see it, smell it. Warplanes sometimes show their red and green lights in a night sky. Engineers and tourists who do not believe in signs sometimes negotiate the unfinished Catalina Highway, but rarely do they get themselves lost into camp.

Civilization upon the island is specialized. There are three hundred men without women. Routine attains the hyper-abnormality common to the military. An hour is never to pass without the sound of a whistle which commands men to walk, eat, sleep, work, play, take laundry, receive mail, stand up and be counted. Life is specialized and it is monastic; monastically drained of sensuality, materialism, zest. Eating serves only to prevent starvation. Sleep begins at a certain moment and ends at a certain moment. You can march into the mess hall desperately hungry but the only pleasure achieved lies in the absence of gnawing stomach. You can sink onto an iron cot exhausted, but the sensual pleasure of rest exists for but a few moments; then has become nothingness until the morning whistle. Prison clothing is anonymous. One's possessions are limited to toothbrush, comb, upper or lower cot, half the space upon a narrow table, a razor. As in jail, the urge to collect possessions is carried to preposterous extents. Rocks, string, knives—anything made by man and forbidden in man's institution—anything,— a red comb, a different kind of toothbrush, a belt—these things are assiduously gathered, jealously hidden or triumphantly displayed. Little sensuality survives in recreation; the inmates' energy has been scientifically and competently sapped by quitting time. What remains is habit, or an echo of habits acquired in real life.

The island's occupants (at this writing) are from unbelievably incongruous environments. Their common bond is, of course, the fact that they were caught. But some of them are as pro-social as others are anti-social. Thirty-one of them are Japanese Americans who refused military service because their Constitutional rights were stolen. There are sixteen Mexican border jumpers who had been enticed into hiking up from as far down as Michococan or Tehuantepec to work in U.S. fields. There are six Hopi Indians who objected politically and religiously—and of course adamantly —to conscription. There are seven Russian Molokans, blond and burly, one Navajo, one Apache (murder), fourteen Negroes, 150 Jehovah's Witnesses, 40 conscientious objectors. Federal Road Camp Number Ten was, as one guard put it, "Interracial as hell." The Nisei arrived sullen, stoic, clannish after half a year in the Denver county jail and after three years in Poston Relocation Camp. In a month, they were the prison's most charming extroverts. The Hopis maintained a cool cynicism about white men after serving two prison terms apiece, or an average of about four or five prison years per man. There also were one Jewish C.O. from Harvard, a Jewish draft evader picked up in Mexico, and four brothers who hid out from the law for a year before the FBI and a posse of 150 men tracked them down and forced surrender. At least 25 colleges were represented among the inmates, and well over a hundred State and Federal prisons and jails could boast that they had graduates in Number Ten.

The only inmate who purchased War Bonds was a man serving five years for defrauding the U.S. Government in a War contract. Few of the Mexicans and Indians spoke English, most of them isolated themselves from the rest of the men. Yet, in the Mess Hall—the only place where segregation was forced— the Negroes were the only inmates made to occupy a separate table. A poll showed that a majority of the men favored immediate abandonment of the practice but various efforts to bring about a change—even an "Interracial Dining Table" where Negroes would sit, and anyone else who wished—were futile. Hunger strikes were planned; the discussions went on for months and several inmates tried sitting with the Negroes. But the majority of CO's rationalized or philosophized that even force would have but transient value.

The dominant emotion of inmates was anguish; hate or fear occured at times but the heavy, hungry suffrage that walked and worked or slept or ate was anguish. It is remarkable that such a force did not have more potent effect; few men had mental breakdowns and were sent away. There was some breaking of rules. Everyone walked out of bounds at one time or another. Four Jehovah's Witnesses built a successful still from ingredients stolen from the culinary department. Petty pilfering was not uncommon. But, just as the average American will steal a nickel while hesitating to steal a hundred dollars the Road Camp inmate stopped short of most crime that wonld cause him to lose his good time.

The attitude of the guards—that is, whatever existed beyond their apathy—was a mixture of bewilderment, admiration and exasperation. One officer, during an argument with a CO, remarked, "You fellows do so much objecting that if we opened the gate right now and told you to go home, some of you would get half way out and then come back and object about that." A few months later, three COs did refuse to leave when their sentences were up. They refused to sign the statement which says that they promise to abide by all laws, knowing they would be drafted again. Two of them refused to accept draft registration cards.

The Jehovah's Witnesses objected to an assignment to cut Christmas trees because Christmas wasn't to be celebrated according to their beliefs. The prison officials gave them special permission to work on the rock crew but insisted that inasmuch as Christmas wasn't to be celebrated, they work as usual on December 25th. Russian Molokans, who cannot eat pork products, were given beef (when meat was available).

All mail was censored but according to convicts who were authorities on incarceration, Federal Road Camp Number Ten allowed more freedom of speech than any other Institution. Not only friends and relatives of Tucson's inmates were informed, but also Civil Liberties groups, the AFSC, several magazines and even Prison Officials in Washington. The Public Relations achievements of prisoners reached an all time high here, though many of the small improvements brought about were good only for the duration of its rôle as a hostel for war objectors.

But despite an advancement in certain liberties; despite the calibre of that year's type of prisoner and a new look worn by the guards, *rehabilitation* appears to have been only average. Nearly all war objectors are still objecting, still belittling the flag, the military, the law. The Witnesses are still witnessing; the Hopis are still going to jail for various offenses. And the mortality on inmates doing time for Federal convictions is still dreadfully high. Probably the reason lies in the fact that rehabilitation is supposed to be brought about by some such miracle as spiritual rebirth.

In actuality, Road Camp Number Ten did little more than protect the inmate from the temptations that resulted in his arrest; shielded him from women to rape, whiskey to drink, automobiles to steal, borders to jump, checks to forge. By shielding him, the prison officials evidently believed they were curing him. But exposure to the good life—the monastic choice—does not necessarily accomplish acceptance. One cannot be forced into a way of life except for a period lasting only as long as the force is applied. Thus, the average inmate, upon release, experimented with all of the sensual pleasures which he had been denied. And the experiment—looked forward to month after month, year after year—was seldom what could be called controlled. Nor was one vocation successfully supplanted by another during incarceration in the desert. Given his choice of forging checks or earning a living by breaking rocks, the inmate would—once the anguish of imprisonment healed —be apt to re-try the former, albeit more scientifically. For nearly all of the occupations here were drudge tasks, bitterly monotonous and oftentimes without purpose. What simply happened is that a lot of men tried *work* for the first time in their lives and found it wanting.

4

When you're in, you dream you are out. When you are out, you dream of being in again. I have been out four years but often

I revisit Federal Road Camp Number Ten during the night—only to make it safely back to my own bedroom by morning. Some of my dreams have achieved the adolescent yearning common to all sufferers; the quickening, saccharine anguish—the bittersweet romanticism of boy without girl, man without freedom, pauper without money. Some of the dreams frighten me awake; one in a nightmare I got *life*, and was returned to Tucson, and got a tremendous ovation, a curious combination of ironic cheers, jeers vomited forth by all unfortunates from the inmates. They were delighted. I loathed seeing them again. They symbolized dreadful trudging days and butterless bread, meatless cooking, long queues for laundry, toothpaste, doctor, soap. I saw the heavy faces and quiet brutality. I saw pig eyes whenever sweets were available. I woke up greedy and heavy with the lead ballast which every prisoner carries in his belly.

Yet, sometimes the unreality of dreaming myself back into prison allowed more happiness than the reality of my present life as a free but felonious individual.

The incarceree dreams of the future. The present is taboo. He daydreams a world blowing its top with pleasures to be drunkenly sampled upon the day of graduation, release, separation, parole, furlough. I looked forward to my own peace, world peace, a plan, a design. All of this was to take place when I got out of prison and all men got out of all armies. There existed hope in unreality. The present has failed to deliver the goods. I can no longer walk the quiet hour before the nine o'clock whistle and believe that the only barrier between myself and freedom is the calendar. I cannot watch the twilight animals come out among the hot rocks and offer to trade places with them. For I see them often now. I am no freer than I was then. They still are free. They do not know that we are going to blow them all to hell some day.

When you are in, your outlook is bent around and turned back or forward. The past is played back in billions of feverish little newsreels which are not truly documentary but edited with an optimism peculiar to U.S. cinema. The present is, of course, extinct. It was too specialized for this environment; it had to die, to be supplanted by something more adapted. Something more adapted was the past or future. Yet, I know now that the future never achieved authenticity. It was an abnormal little daydream, a scheme cunningly contrived. I never once believe that on November 23, 1944, I was going to walk out of prison.

What could happen to prevent this?

Here logic gives way to superstition. Superstition sleeps with frustration. It shares frustration with anguish, fear, anger. I knew that a rock would fall upon me sometime between now and Dressing Out day; that a truck, driven by a wheelhappy Jehovah's Witness would experience a kind of Armegeddon and all aboard would be killed. The heart might simply cease to beat. A Federal Man with handcuffs might take you into custody on the day of departure; what did you know about the crime on the night of the 27th, 1939?

But you have committed no other crime.

No, you have committed innumerable crimes.

Overparking. Speeding. Intimate relations, disturbance, a swimming hole, stolen candy bar, 1925. Gold watch you found in a vacant lot. Logic says these are not candidates. They occurred too long ago; there is no proof. Superstition is your mistress. She says that technically you still are guilty. FBI has your records, keeps adding to its files. Once in you're labeled. Another arrest, another trial, another conviction?

The future then has little to say.

It can fictionalize a free man, fishing in a California trout stream, May first, 1945. Exactly 432 miles from this pool a whistle blows, calling the men to count. But the vibrations of its order are tempered by other sound waves and the angler makes his cast while dead men in denims line up before the guards.

But the future can only guess about the future. It cannot guarantee your proximity beside the pool which lies only 94 time-days away. The future can take you on logical trips into the past; you were, after all, there. Thus, when it takes you upon innumerable trips which are stamped 1945; post prison—it really is travelling roads used prior to 1944. Every road turns out to be one you've travelled before.

I avert my gaze from the present. I cannot look it in the eye. My eyes look intelligent only when they see backwards.

How do I know that I am out and not in?

Once in, you dreamed you were out.

There were cozy little events during the night. They were sheared by the whistle, riding chilly black air. There were groans and fuzzy heartache and the deadening awareness that you are here, and not there.

I write this believing that I am out.

I am four hundred miles from the whistle right now.

There is no proof of this.

I had veal chops last night. I went fishing yesterday. An old friend from prison visited me Tuesday. My wife doesn't like COs. The three of us talked. He and I had much in common within prison bounds. We seem to have parted now. I am not sure about any of these things. The whistle may be only 50 yards from me now. It may be getting ready to blow through its top. If it does, may do likewise. The barracks lights will flash, iron cots will squeak, I will have dreamed that I dreamed that I dreamed I was out when I was in for the hundredth time.

Have I actually dreamed that I dreamed I was in when I was out?

Have I dreamed that I paid $8500 for a house assessed for $200 just a year ago. If I am dreaming that the hundreds of warplanes across the bay are warming up for world war three, then my loss is the world's gain.

I resent the insecurity of dreams. Maybe I am dreaming that I write of my prison experiences whereas, in reality, I was an officer in the Navy and came home highly decorated. I may still be in the San Diego County jail, awaiting shipment to prison. I may be waiting for my number to be called and, if so, I fear my decision. Will conscience win? Did it win? I have experienced evil.

Had I not experienced it, I could only invent pleasant dreams. But now that I have permitted fear—now that I have entertained suspicion, feted anger, plotted with hate, slept with superstition —now that I have been in and out—I am a plaything for the dream. I never should have beat my dog in 1928 and hated George Fulkerson. That made my prison dream possible. But I have no proof that I have been fingerprinted and cannot vote. The burden of proof lies upon the courts.

MCNEIL ISLAND

DON DEVAULT

PERSONALITIES ...There was a man from Alaska. He was middle age, quite good looking. He had probably got drunk and robbed a store or something. I don't remember just what he was in for. He was white (though tanned heavily by the weather) and about 5 ft. 8 in. tall, medium weight. I don't know whether he could read and write or not. I think he could, but not very well. However, his lack of education was not from being slow or stupid. He was, rather, quite excitable and energetic. His speech and I guess his background was American, although I believe he could speak some Italian. He was fairly good natured except in argument when he could be very dogmatic. His attitude on COs was rather contradictory. He mostly didn't like them but apparently came to make exceptions. He seemed to like to argue religion with the JWs at which times both sides would get very hot under the collar and be about ready to jump at each others' throats. Such arguments were even known to keep him and a group of JWs out on project for some time after quitting time. He sang in choir with us. The most remarkable thing that he did, however, was to build a violin in about two weeks time just before he went out. He had made about 20 violins before on the outside just as a hobby. An old 'Sourdough' had made himself a violin on the prison farm there when they had forbidden him to bring one out from the mainline with him. When 'Sour-dough' went out, the man that I am describing took measurements from Sourdough's violin and went to work on his own, using wood that he found around the place and a few tools, clamps, glue, etc. that he managed to sneak in from the shops. He took great pride in telling onlookers how to select the wood, what proportions to use for the best sound effects, etc. He painted it black for lack of better material. The finished violin had excellent tone. One fellow who had had some concert experience said it seemed to have everything that a good concert violin ought to have. (Old Sourdough's violin had been very squeaky.) The maker said that it's largely luck how a violin turns out, and that time may change this one. He could not read music but he could play well by ear, and delighted in playing old-fashioned hoe-downs. etc. Then he did all he could to get as many others in the place to make violins also, promising them advice. By the time he went out there were four or five more violins under construction by COs and JWs.

There was an old Indian, a Blackfoot, from Montana, very tall, light-skinned, grey-haired, about 60 years old. He was very quiet and resigned to his fate, though not at all happy about it. He did not talk much to people but I got to know him quite well by bunking next to him, refraining from asking him personal questions, getting him tobacco and candy at commissary. He would bring me contraband Brazil nuts, peanuts, cookies. Like most full-blooded Indians he did not grow any beard, and so he gave me the shaving equipment that he had been issued. He liked to read cowboy stories and see that kind of movie, but would complain about how they represented the Indians, complaining mostly that they did not attribute any intelligence to the Indians. Once when the camp was getting crowded he said he supposed that all the Indians and Negroes would soon be put in the barn. Otherwise, however, he was quite pleasant in a dignified sort of way. He had ridden horseback all his life, and his job on the farm was caretaker of the horses. In Montana he had owned a rodeo (as apparently very many Indians there do) putting on horse shows for tourists at frequent intervals. I don't know what he was in for but from various hints it might have been some sort of meat-marking deal, using a gov't stamp without having the meat officially inspected, or something like that. There may also have been some murder or attack mixed up with it. He had been in for several years already and had lost everything he ever owned. He talked as though he expected to get out again but I don't think that it was to be very soon. I think he had ten or 20 years or so. He spoke English well, which is not true of all the Indians.

A little Eskimo from Alaska used to recite to every newcomer (until they started coming in too fast) the story of his airplane ride from Alaska and how bad the jail was at Juneau where they had to stop over. He smoked big cigars that gave the impression of being half as big as he, lost his temper easily, had a tendency to swagger, spoke English quite well and in that respect was star pupil in the reading class. He sang in the choir (which was not selected for quality of voice) but threatened to quit when on trips to the inside we had to wait around for the truck before coming back and were late for dinner. In general he had the naïve, selfish morality of a child, but would swear and talk like a grown-up. Everybody liked him however, partly because they couldn't take him seriously.

There was a Negro-Spanish fellow... He was born in Puerto Rico, and brought to Harlem, N.Y. at the age of 2, and brought up there. He had joined the navy to impress a girl friend and served as cook on a submarine through some dangerous missions. Selling a Navy telescope was what got him to McNeil. He always listed his race as Puerto Rican and refused to recognize race problems or the existence of a problem in Puerto Rico. He had the quite typical (I think) N.Y. philosophy of openly proclaiming "me for myself." He mixed mostly with the intellectual COs that he came in with because, I guess, they seemed to like him, and he often contributed some worth while, albeit uncultured, gems to the discussions, but mostly seemed to get lost in the more sophisticated CO discussions, which I don't blame him for. After a couple months he insulted a guard and was bugged (sent to the mental ward of the hospital in the mainline, which was the only way that officials could send men with 'county jail' or P. camp sentences into the main-line of the Penitentiary, for punishment purposes.) Other than the idea of the thing, I do not know that there was any very bad maltreatment practiced in the Psychoneurotic ward at McNeil Island. This fellow got out after his sentence of a few months was served and in San Francisco...got into jail for another month or two there on a completely framed up charge. Then, after serving that he was caught wearing his navy uniform again, which he is not supposed to do and has been sent back up to McNeil Island.

...   .

GUARDS The guards are not allowed to carry guns. The only guns on McNeil Island were in the towers surrounding the 'main-line'.

There was a fair amount of congeniality between guards and inmates, although both sides stayed in their own places pretty well. For example, one of the guards that was fairly well liked by most of the inmates got to talking with me. He had attended Missouri State Teachers College and knew a couple of students there whom I got to know very well in California. However, I cut the conversation off myself, because I wanted it to be plain, especially to the other inmates, that I was with the inmates if any controversies should arise. Mostly the guards and inmates worked out arrangements that made life easiest for both. The boss of the orchard crew was not exactly a guard and did not wear a uniform but was hired to manage the orchards as an expert. He was a real gentleman and so nice that one could not help being friendly with him. He never complained about anyone's work and treated the inmates as men.

Another one, who managed the crops and machinery, had no respect for cons (or for anybody else, much) and would like to have been more of a slave driver than the general slow pace of prison work would let him be. Inexperienced guards were usually the worst ones. After the cons had broken them in they weren't so bad. Usually they did not have college background. Many were quite old. One young one was son of a man who had owned land on McNeil Island before the gov't bought it all up. Usually the cons knew more about the work being done than the guards did, and much of the work around the prison could not have been done or even directed by the guards or anyone in the administration except for brainwork or knowledge contributed by cons.

ADMINISTRATION The last sentence about relative competence of cons and guards along technical lines goes for the administration too, and when the administration failed to recognize it and would insist on doing some things in an inferior way it made for friction and discontent. I am allowing, of course, for some cases where the cons just thought they knew better than the gov't men. However, the administration often let the cons do specialized work in their own way so that there was not always friction.

As with guards and inmates the administration included all kinds of people. The farm superintendent who was there when I first came was disliked by almost everyone. A typical bureaucrat, he worked from the rule book, bullied inferiors and kow-towed extensively to superiors. Besides that he seemed to hate to see anyone comfortable. One Sunday a group of about five of us were listening to the NBC concert over the radio in the recreation room while almost everyone else had gone in with the truck to the mainline to see the baseball game. One of the fellows was lying down on the the wooden bench while listening. The superintendent came in and said, "S......s, if want to lie down go lie on your bunk." He posted a notice prohibiting inmates from making picture frames out of match-sticks (an art that had grown up) "because some inmates had been found using contraband materials in their construction." He tried to stop orchard crew members from bringing fruit in to other inmates, although the orchard manager didn't mind the practice. He was a young fellow working for promotion and the cleanliness and orderliness of the dorms at the times that the warden came over from the mainline for inspection were of much greater importance than rehabilitation of a bunch of cons.

His successor when the Farm was officially changed to a 'Prison Camp' was almost an exact opposite. He was T. J. Brock and moved in with the Dupont (Wash.) road camp. Brock was just as firm in his orders and all that, but he had much less regard for rules and more regard for actual welfare of the men. (In line with this same characteristic he was also harder to get at because of his more irregular office hours.) It is reported that at Dupont once Brock had received notice from State police that they wanted a prisoner who was due to be released soon and would he please hold the fellow if they didn't get there soon enough. When the release date came Brock let the fellow out at 1 minute after midnight and took him to the highway where he could hitch-hike his way out of the state before the police came. Brock was quite willing to listen to COs' problems (although he was a Legionnaire) and the guards under him overlooked things that the inmates did as much as they could and still maintain their authority. Brock did not get along too well with his superiors particularly when he was so close to them as on the Island and so he was preparing to take charge of the Columbia-Dupont honor camp that was being set up in eastern Washington, when I left.

The first Farm supervisor mentioned above put many restrictions on educational work, all of which was done after work hours. He would not let me use any apparatus in my class on electricity, although what I wanted was simple and available, simply because he didn't want a mess to be made. Neither would he let the dining room or the dressing room for the showers be used as class room, although class room was badly needed. Brock or his subordinates did allow these to be used as class rooms.

... ...

RECREATION A good deal of recreation such as bull-sessions went on during work hours. However, the regular time for recreation was after supper from about 5:30 PM to about 9:00 PM. As much of this time as there was daylight in could be spent outdoors in the vicinity of the dormitories. Baseball, handball, volley ball and basket ball and horseshoes were the chief outdoor sports. Indoors it was mostly dominoes with some checkers and chess. Also rug-making, reading books, listening to the radio, arguing, etc.

... ...

FOOD The food is practically never satisfactory in any boarding house. How much of the very great dissatisfaction expressed over the food in prison is due merely to a general dislike for the whole place, is hard to say. It is true that mental attitudes can affect appetites and vice versa. New arrivals at McNeil were generally pleased with the food for a few days. Indeed it did have good variety throughout the week, and considering war shortages, seemed to me about as good as could be expected. However each week was repeated almost identically and it got very tiresome after about the tenth time......

It helped the food situation a lot to be working on the orchard crew during the fruit-picking season. We had all the fruit we could eat there and brought in much to other inmates. It helped also to be on the repair crew later as we could go up to the chicken house to fix up the wiring and boil ourselves an egg at the same time, or go to the kitchen to repair the sink and get a hamburger fried by the cooks, when no one was looking or maybe an extra bottle of milk. Out of pure friendliness to the repair crew the orchard manager kept the repair shop stocked with boxes of apples during the winter (also strictly undercover of course). Apples, oranges, grapefruit and candy could be gotten at the commissary if one had money.

... ...

LETTERS Some fellows felt the restrictions on quantity of letters that could be written (2 per week) or received (7 or 9 per week). To me it was a great relief. Not many at McNeil seemed to feel the censorship of contents very much, except those that particularly wanted to air grievances about the prison system. Political opinions did not seem to receive censorship at McNeil. Mostly letters were censored only when they specifically infringed one of about ten specific items printed on the rejection slip. For example, I had a letter rejected because I asked in it that my mother copy my letters and send them around to my friends. The censor said this disobeyed the regulation about trying to communicate with unauthorized correspondents thru authorized ones. However, when I rewrote the letter I said in it to my mother that I had found out, via the route of writing it in a letter and having it rejected, that I was not supposed to have her copy my letters over to send to others, and that I did not want to break the rules, etc. That passed the censor all right! Furthermore, my mother continually quoted letters addressed to me and written to her and did it completely openly and all were allowed in. I would answer by simply talking *about* the unauthorized correspondent rather than saying, "Write to...". For reasons of this sort we at McNeil did not take the letter censorship very seriously and tended to be amused by word of the Lewisburg strike which reached us just a little before I went out.

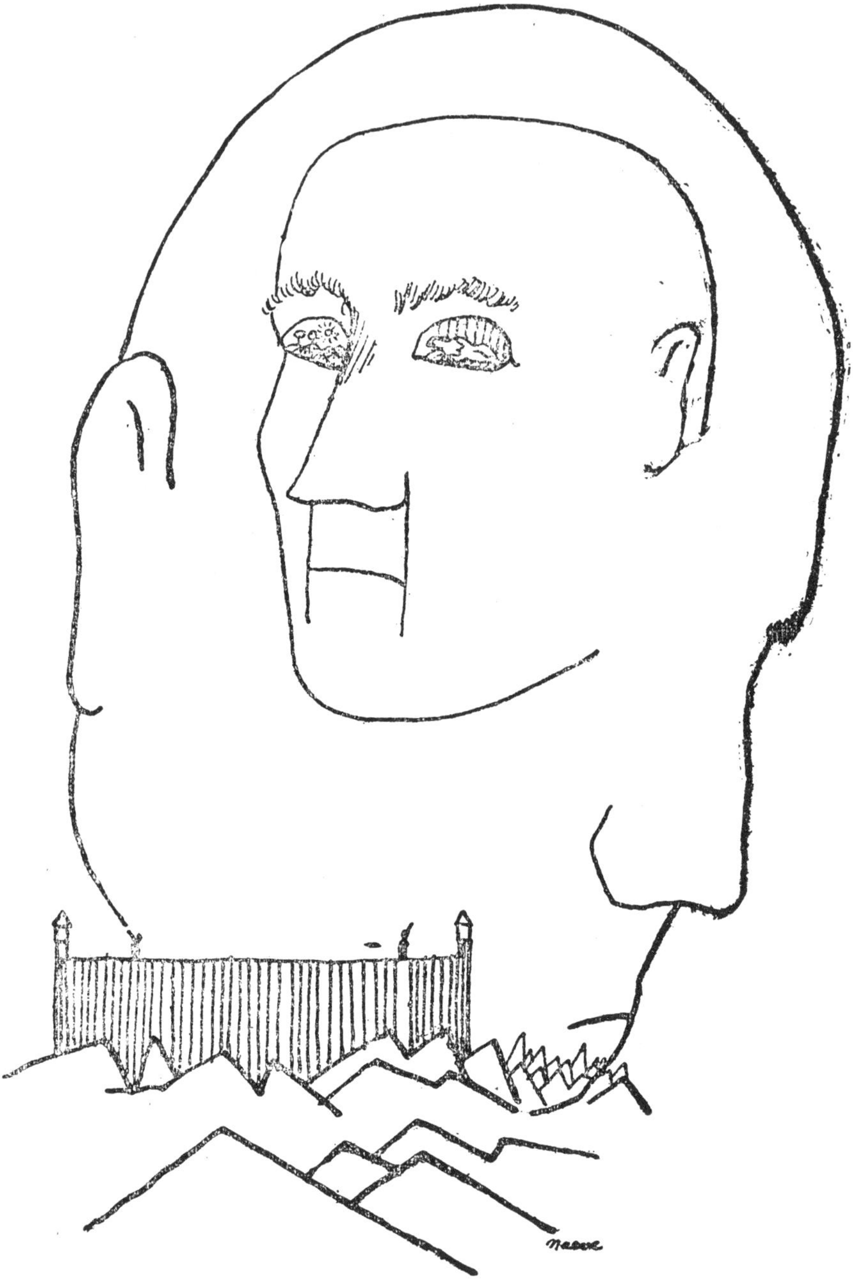

NOTES ON THE PRISON COMMUNITY

BERNARD PHILLIPS

A. RECRUITMENT

Prisons are the least-mentioned institutions of the state. Just as one becomes a responsible citizen through learning that nakedness is bad, that elimination should be secret, that masturbation is unspeakably dangerous, so one is led to believe that the prison system is the indispensable but unmentionable cloacal region of the "community". Stereotypes about criminality and criminals utilize much the same terms and ideas as those about sexual perversion, or any other structure associated with nastiness and revulsion, contrary to good taste.

...It is valuable to study the prison community not because it varies sharply from the general community, but because it is a total psycho-social organization in a condition of isolation from minor crises of the general society. It is the image of general community, a clean mirror unsullied by the breath of public attention. Truly, an extension of the metropolis, remodeled by its inhabitants to make it better for them than the life they lead "outside". There could be no rejection of the outside, anyway, for its denizens enter daily emphasizing the nearness, and granting as privileges direct contact with the general community—non-prison foods, conveniences, cultural objects (books, radio).

Authoritarian standards implicit in the general community are unmasked in the prison. Power-wielders are clearly defined, as are the limitations of their constructivity, in their own inefficiency. The controlled are very important to the controllers, they are watched, counted and recounted, studied....

Prisons and armies are laboratories for perfecting and smoothing class-authoritarian techniques. The prison, administratively considered, remains despite innovations an extension of the police force and fulfills in an ordered and contained space the funtions of police power in an unordered space.

CONTROLLERS AND CONTROLLED

The criterion of police efficiency is that no activity of any group or individual should escape scrutiny, and that there is sufficient arsenal and manpower on hand to stop any group or individual activity at the command of constituted authority. The problem for the cop, in the gun tower or at the picket line, is whether or not to take initiative to intervene. Bluntly put, the cop is beyond all law and restraint except for learned morality. So long as he goes by the manual (a flexible document) there are no limits to his action. He is not punished for simple error (infinitely extensible catagory!) unless he seriously misjudges the latent resources of the person he accosts. Justice costs heavily in time and money, and if the cop has any powers of observation at all he will select appropriate arrestees, inside or out.

The psychology of police work is not that of unremitting vigilance (so much has to be overlooked), but it is *waiting and assaulting*.✦ It is more obvious when the cop is working in a closed space. His reactions in this situation impose special problems on inmates accustomed to rigid routinization, and initiate spasmodic reactions on their part. Man-watching is a nerve-wracking and exacting task

---

✦ The rationale of police work reaches its essence in the guards who wait in hiding, then leap out and club any passing convict. The element of surprise adds much to their pleasure. A disciplinary board for guards has slightly reduced the quantum of 'assaulting' More prominent are the controllers who try to pick fights with the unwilling prisoners.

even when the watcher is a competent individual with some reason to feel superiority to his charges. However, the ordinary prison guard cannot feel this generalized self assurance. Many of his charges are obviously superior to him in intelligence, social effectiveness, or education.* His learned morality often leads him to anxiety about punishment of innocent men. The tendancy is to be "as decent as possible", although the employee's manual instructs him never to debase himself by being familiar with the inmates. As compensation for this illicit intersubjectivity, the guard persecutes the inferior human specimens who are inevitably components in a prison populace.

GENERAL STRUCTURE

The prison contains two great collectives with 1. distinct and non-transponible memberships, 2. recruited from homogeneous social and distinct psychological types, 3. maintaining definite tension and conflict with the alter-collectivity. Their differentiation is along typical and ethical lines, sharply dividing the inmate population into two in-groups (equal, or almost so, in numbers).

The *rats* are inmates who have frankly made a living out of crimes against property. They are the robbers, burglers, and the professional thieves. Among this group the adage 'honor among thieves' holds. The rats have a conscious justification for their life-ways—hatred of work, love of novelty, travel, adventure, resentment of social constraint which concretely means proletarianization. Many have supported wives and families with the proceeds from their depredations. Characteristically the rats are adequate persons, readily prisonized, logical, generous, argumentative. They take the roles of leaders and constructive agitators. Their criteria for acceptance or rejection of new inmates are positive, non-economic

* The prison mail office illustrates the extreme low in mentality. It is difficult to get a letter past the censors if any literary expression is used, or any word of more than four syllables. For instance, the writer had one letter returned with a red circle around the word 'aposiopesis', with the threatening comment--"Any further vulgar language and we will cancel your mail privileges". Poor 'parataxis' later met the same fate.

and post-juvenile.

Squarejohns are offenders against the person (except for those instances where the rats' occupational hazards of gun-using have resulted in inadvertant slaying). They include the sex offenders of all kinds, impulse-and-regret murderers, subnormal and inadequate personalities ('dopes' and 'goons'), and numerous 'frauds' convicted for forgery, insufficient funds or other business trickery.

The crime is the personal comment on the world. Not everyone is capable of every crime, and there are rats who have never offended against the person no matter how powerful the push of circumstance and opportunity. The reaction of the prisoner is *a posteriori* proof of the nature and reality of the offense. Innocent men and rats do not bellyache. Squarejohns do. Preoccupations also are consonant with the crime. The rat, thinking of future release, wonders whether anybody has cased that good job in Peoria, while the squarejohn wonders if he can get away with it with his next daughter and calculates how old she will be then.

One would call this merely ethical differentiation if it were only a matter of one sort of criminal defending 'his' kind of crime and denouncing the 'opposition' for committing another type of crime. However, the difference can be regarded as structural, because the squarejohns carry the pattern of personal violence through in their day-to-day relations with their own and other types. They are more prone to show object-aggression, and often this becomes apparent in relation to inanimate objects too—squarejohns burn mattresses, smash radios and light bulbs, stuff up the plumbing system when they are excited.

Socially, the 'sqarejohns' are the good citizens who maintain the ethics of the general community, as against the rats' defiance of the code. This is the basal paradox (?) and central point of conflict among the inmate population, an absolute contrariety to all the assumptions of the meliorist and reformatory strategy so loudly espoused by the 'curing' school among positivist penologists. Those individuals who look and sound the best to the parole boards are the ones who *do* constitute an actual, walking physical threat in the absence of supervision—while the 'bad-risk', serial-offender 'tough' is the individual who could, without supervision, reintegrate in the general community easily and without emotional disturbance because of his achieved self-distanciation from the unstable moral codes.

A facile characterization of the whole squarejohn complex would be—conscious guilt, repentance, active striving toward social recognition and unconditional reinstatement, The johns tend to be older men with unconcealable mental and physical deficiencies, and correspondingly strong reliance on communal sanctions, often with concentrated avoidance of actions to which their abnormalities bring them close. With increasing age they show more rigid scrupulosity in obedience to precepts of religion, patriotism, and other introcepted codes and props for concealment of constitutional pathologies. Any person who reveals a dependent and inadequate personality is classified in the prison as a squarejohn, and this fact of forcible classification is especially offensive to the good citizens who wish to regain ethical solidarity with the outside community, and fail to see the identity of their moralizing and the behaviour of the feeble-minded who are driven into association with them.

The rats, utilitarians and hedonists as they are, feel that the only bar to their success is the process of law enforcement.

In prison where their welfare cannot be advanced by pursuing random ends, but *can* be supported by collective action of the regime of moods dubbed "prisonization", they maintain a peace-tending society which is more effective for securing their group welfare than those available to them in the general community, in part because of the limitations of ends imposed, the advantageous immediacy of concrete individual interaction, and the pre-exposure of alien caste ethics and counter-claims.

This contrast of the two collectivities does not imply that a reversal of function has taken place inside the prison, with the outlaws taking social initiative because the good citizens are prostrated in masochism or *anomie*. The process is more complex, and is known as prisonization.

BASIC DEMANDS

The presumption of the inexperienced is that the prisoner is under tremendous pressures, that peculiar distortions of personality must appear, that social adjustments would be below the norms of a "free" community, that pathological reactions would be formed to the constant authoritarian environment, and radiate beyond those affected. This is the romantic perspective of the humanitarian citizen or the typical social scientist—that perennial orthopsychiatrist.

However the main effect upon the individual prisoner is that he becomes "prisonized"! This is supposedly shown by increased passivity and greater submission to authority, by changes in the gradient of receptivity (toward or away from 'socially worth-while goals')—in general, by heightened suggestibility to stimuli provided both by his associates and by 'society'.

This interpretation of the prisonization process presumes that discipline in the prison is constructive. However, one cannot measure the prisoner's conduct by his conduct record, because the authority (which he either breaches or does not) is coercive, not constructive. Most problems of discipline arise from trying to feed and house many men where there is room for only few. Breakdown in authority is not a measure of inmate performance but of the laziness and stupidity of the "administration". A great part of misconduct is constructive rebellion against impossible conditions.

For instance, one main effort of "authority" is enforcement of physical filthiness for inmates. Cells have no warm water, washing personal clothing is limited to 10 minutes one day per week, washing state clothes is forbidden (the very best that can be hoped for is a weekly change.) The state's soap *will* clean, but it also takes away the skin, one thin hand towel (16 x 29 inches) is issued each week—and must be used for the weekly 10 minute shower bath, too. About a third of all rule infractions for which inmates are sentenced by "summary court" are those which arise from men sneaking a bath (or semi-bath), washing state clothing, or bargaining for haircuts, for laundry service, etc. Because cell sinks drain at hourglass speed everyone must wash up in the toilet bowl—washing is therefore a rare and reluctant process. Rules of order enforced by convicts are made to break down or evade such conditions wherever possible. The conflicts of ethics and status between rat and squarejohn are eliminated by brute necessity. One may dislike the crippled, grizzled sodomist, but if he can get the laundry 'fixed' one perforce deals with him.

Geniality and solidarity of the inmate caste rest upon this immediate basis of coöperative rule-breaking and exchanging favors. The mechanical and anonymous regime is not adjusted to humane needs, though it ensures animal survival. Communication for interest serving is taboo, so that all humane response is also rule-breaking. Commands are depreciated by the convict, they appear not worth following. No initiative has been left to the inmate, such would be a threat to 'security.' Since nothing done in the prison is directed to any rational or productive end, there is no formal freedom for the prisoner to perform meaningful actions. Thus like the citizen on the street he is coerced (or persuaded) to perform nonsense activity. The only difference arises from the fact that the citizen has formal freedom (some command-following may lead to rational conclusion, while situationally, he finds that his power of personal initiative is meaningless). So the convict follows commands, tempering obedience with contempt for uniformed authority which is creating such a fuss, shouting so loudly, looking over its shoulder in unnecessary uneasiness. The convict regards guard behaviors as interjections of a strange sort of animal caught in the web of his own conduct. Realization of this reciprocity is the subjective sign of prisonization.

The objective index of prisonization is that the inmate is affiliated with one or the other of the ethical collectivities and defends its values. It is quite possible for two rats and two 'johns' to share the same cell for years without any relations other than contractual (economic) or caste-directed (rule-breaking). The situation cannot be altered by authority, and the tendency is for squarejohns to gravitate to idle companies (a correlate of age, ill-health and social inadequacy as much as of outraged inability to defend good citizenship against the logical jibes of the rats).

With the inmate's loss of formal freedom to approve or disapprove of plans, authoritarian behavior becomes completely irrelevant to those who are not immediate victims of the caprice, and the inmate turns to the community of his kind. The introversion is not toward the lowest norms of association represented. Scrupulous courtesy is necessary where nobody has freedom to release energy except under the scrutiny of three other men in a 9x11 cell. The trouble maker is frozen out as soon as possible, and no great sympathy is felt for the extreme deviate in his segregated quarters, for in nine cases out of ten he was engineered there by collective repression of inmates. The loud agitator must go to preserve the equilibrium of both the adequate and inadequate person. There is nothing more pitiful or disgusting than to be in a cell and hear a stream of blasphemy or a chant of innocence, when minor irritations have summated to the point where one is ready to indulge in the same behavior—if it were not for having associates who would react violently against, and depersonalize, even such an expression. Depersonalization and equanimity are sought for between inmates. Trouble of any sort can only mean trouble for them.

When everyone wears the same clothing, eats the same food at the same time and place, sleeps in identical beds, in identical rooms, for the same number of hours, and goes to work that is equally unremunerative and uninteresting and unimportant, conflicts between men largely thin down to invarients of social interaction. The organization of activity is not exhausted in object aggressions and manipulations, but develops nuances of individuation. There is heightening of individuality wherever possible, but the limits of this possibility are drawn very tightly, *not by impersonal but by personal forces*. One does not have to guess how business will turn out, or what the boss thinks of one's personality or output. The 'business' is recognizably of no value, and for the subjectivity questions one can secure a ready answer since the boss is always in sight, always carries a club, and is trained to despise *you*. The only difference from "outside" is that here all these relationships are transparent: the paycheck and the theory of courtesy do not obscure interaction between distinct social classes. The displacement of courtesy and convention between convict and keeper would be almost sufficient in itself to intensify display of these forms as between convicts. Learned codes of taste are infused with new life when they facilitate responses to extreme behavior and extreme situations. A partial prescription for reactions to extreme situations lessens tensions and indicates prisonization. One will dispose of the stabber's knife as a mark of courtesy and friendly concealment, as one wipes away the spilled drink of one's guest.

Prisonization, then, is accomodation to out-caste status with active reservation of a distinct ethical position. Primacy must be granted to rule-breaking as the vehicle for caste association. While self-justification is a tempting form of action, it is limited to the squarejohns, for all practical purposes—as a sign of enlistment in *their* collectivity of thwarted good citizenship. Self justification is an incomplete tampon to object or environmental aggression. For the entire caste prisonization is the measure (in the varying forms of introversion and socialization) of adequacy and self-integration which recognizes that general end-following is inappropriate to the social situation. The individual with any social capabilities whatever will make a rapid adjustment to the conditions of unspectacular comradeship in one or the other collectivity. Initiation is by example. Extremes of courtesy, concern, solicitude, at first do give the impression of homosexual overture or pathological reaction. But they are the symptoms of a softened and gentled life and the goodwill is real. The novice interprets special services as special acts of friendship, and then suddenly finds himself going out of the way to do favors for some stranger, often at personal risk. One is always thereafter "giving time" to others—and gladly. Message giving and general coördination devolve as tasks for the range-man who serves several cells in a single range and arranges barter and exchange. Highly socialized persons seek these jobs, and others such as library deilvery boy and mail and commissary delivery. One does not need many close friends: almost anyone who is free enough to reach one's cell will run errands and do jobs which 'outside' would be entrusted only to close friends. If he does not, he cannot last long on his pleasant assignment before getting into trouble.

AFTER PRISONIZATION

...The convict is always in a hurry—one created by himself —and quite oblivious of the fact that he is rushing in circles. Environmental sameness invests every action with special significance, brevity and uncertainty of friendly contacts makes for infinite planning and replanning of what to do and say in any particular instant, how to bring that instant about, how to preserve inconspicuosity during it...Meanwhile there is time and more time to be filled. One can race with time, by doing this, and this, and... Spasmodicity becomes the way of life, the restless behavior of the untrained or mistrained person, with components of irritability, anxiety, misdirected or briefly sustained effort. The escape patterns of the weakly motivated individual often closely resemble the states of overwork or job-fatigue of the strongly motivated and usually productive person. Watch the inmate in the dormitory after the day's work. He reads, rushes to a friend's bunk to chat avidly, goes by the card tables and stays for one hand with a casual group, takes a shower, types a letter, reads again, walks swiftly around the whole dormitory a few times, smuggles, makes and distributes a round of tea, then revises his letter, etc., etc. No activities last longer than nine minutes, few less than four. Multiply this behavior by 150 (the number of men in the dormitory) and it is evident that a report on it must reveal either a sociometric chaos or a smoothly functioning community in which the individual has a low but definite and constant stimulus 'value' for his associates. The latter is the case......

THE RESERVE-MECHANISMS

...All activities introverted toward the prison community make for a radical split between johns and rats. There is active conflict over the recruitment to the collectivities of the new prisoners ('fish'). The squarejohn is not a good argument for his own ethical code, and it is one repulsive to the young offender fresh from strife against it—but the mechanism of the sexual lure is very powerful. If one will only believe in God and country, he can re-stabilize his sexual life, and this is a powerful attraction for the young man. On the other hand, general courtesy, services, and sociability are provided by the rats. The young man thus undergoes a long period of 'wavering' between standards—but has to come down on one side or the other, or be outlawed by everybody. Contrary to public opinion about the mixture of young offenders with 'hardened criminals', the hardened criminals often accept the youth as a guest and transient, who is to be converted *from* criminal activity. "Bub, look at us,—it doesn't pay..." is the pattern of much recruiting-speech. Rats mute their own extraordinary opinions and convert many youngsters to the ideal of conformity —"for your own sake, you're young and can still choose." The dangers, physical and mental, are, for youth, not offered by the 'radicals' or rats, but by the good citizens. This is again a reproduction of the situation "outside".

INDIVIDUATION

Material for individuality is strictly limited. Every new inmate learns to dog-face, that is to assume an apathetic, *characterless* facial expression and posture when viewed by authority. The dog-face is acquired easily when everyone freezes or relaxes into inmobility. The face is that typical of streets, of social occassions, of all concealment. Relaxation comes when inmates are alone: there is an exaggeration of the smiling effervescence of the 'friendly' party. The face that is protective by day is aggressively hardened and hate-filled by night, against the stationed or pacing guard. Tensity and dislike follow assumption of the face, guards react with scrupulous relaxedness, holding the face "soft" with an effort often accompanied by slight trembling of hands.

How to express contempt for authority? The manner of 'obeying' orders is one way. Resentful alacrity is most common. A dormitory group accustomed to marching into the dining hall in single file, with men finding positions beside their friends, was ordered to march into the hall double-file. (Cell block companies have set order for marching and seating...) After a great deal of scowling and muttering from men hurried from the dormitary, a double line was formed. Thereafter the unpopular guard who first gave the order was always confronted by formation of a double-file line, although a single trial had convinced him of the inconvenience caused to other company guards by his innovation. He did not attempt to reverse his order, and within two weeks every guard who was especially disliked found that the inmates formed double lines for him. The practice spread to another dormitory. Negroes are especially apt at parody, sometimes breaking into a goose-step. They seat themselves at table 10 at a time, snatching off caps simultaneously and precisely.

Individuation, being impossible on the level of consumption and standards of comfort, develops as ego-strengthening eccentricity. Patterns of eccentricity then fade into desultory acts (with spectators) or circular forms, very unusual in content, but conscious and definitely designed! Spasmosdicity favors the apparently desultory act (coenopportune reaction). Examples include *hectoring* and *pseudo-sales*: going into the dining hall, where talk in line is prohibited, one man will stand aside and chant "Get your programs here, meal programs right here, one dime—can't tell one dish from another without a program—also a list of everything served in this room—five lines 10 cents." The largest sale in 1946 was for Braino: "Clear that clogged brain with Braino, one great truth, fi' cents!" The truth enjoined as Braino was: "All people are just people. Don't let any people tell you they aren't people."

Hectoring usually produces audience response disregarding any threats of interferance from authority, and is directed at least obliquely against authoritarianism. Companies saddled with especially oppressive guards show great increase in overt individuation of the mens' conduct, and attempts to discipline the "hectors" leads to booing the guard (with resultant collective punishment).

NORMS OF DISORDER

The most striking aspect of criminal thought is the universal maintainance of the "sacredness of the individual". How is it that the social type which orients itself toward aggression against other individuals and their interests should maintain this ideology? Is the conviction simply a verbal attitude arising from imprisonment with its loss of social status, or a factor in the motivation of criminal behavior?

The rat has a profound belief that the people he dubs "citizens" in the prison populace are identical with the man-on-the-street whom the rat robs and dubs "sucker". Note that the citizen or squarejohn is the individual who is spending either a very brief or a very long time in prison, as punishment for an offense either "trivial" or "very serious". He is the non-repeater, typically, or an older man whose offense was simple index of senility, The rat is a serial offender who totals up years in prisons, jails, and workhouses, and lacks any strong familial or friendship-ties in the community. He is confined inside and outside to social and "business" relationships with other rats. Exigencies of escape often lead one rat to betray another, indeed *informing* is the characteristic sin of the trapped rat.

The convict can always point to the man on the streets and say truthfully: "He put me here." Rats are vengeful and scornful of all morality—relying on anybody has always meant catastrophe to them. [Objectively, many rats are orphans or neglected children, have never had a family life, are ready to repeat the pattern of illigitimacy-and-abandonment which is the model "background"...]

The "citizen" wants out, to renew his old associations and

to attempt to pick up living again where he left off. The prison is to him a social blank, not the place where he finds his old friends. Actually his offenses indicate that rejoining the community will be less easy than he dreams—he is often intellectually and physically inadequate, attracted to old associations which have damaged him in the past. But, emotionally dependent and deficient in self-analysis as he is, the citizen is pointed away from prisonization. The world beyond is habitable and interesting.

The rat is really infuriated by the conservatism and religiosity of the older offenders and sex-criminals. He does not perceive that these uneducated men have no other theory of motivation and conduct which has 'prestige' in their social circle, and that they will cling to it under the insults of the rats. Further the content of Christian doctrine is excellent solace for anyone wishing to justify what he recognizes (with his critics) as irrational action. The essential plea is that the individual is helpless as against his own affectual makeup. Human nature is sinful, anybody will slip once in a while, I don't think it would happen again. "I have paid my debt to society, don't you think they should let me out?"

Convicts are by no means ethically agnostic. The agreement on what it is 'ethical' to do, does serve to define one's position in the rat or citizen collectivities—'ethics' and 'personality' are perhaps the most-overworked words in the prison, nuances in their definition give the trained observer basis for prognosis of the speaker's future, when his actual offense and his speaking circle are known.

Rats deny validity of retribution for their aggressions on two contrary grounds: 1. "Nothing I ever do hurts the common people..." 2. "Somebody ought to ball up those lunchbucket artists, those staunch citizens..." Part of their interest in continuing criminality is that it causes real and observable damage to the interests of others. But the rat often uses the Robin Hood agument, saying that he redistributes property among his friends (who need it most) and that none of his exploitations work hardships comparable to those imposed by "lunchbucket life".

Each group envisions *personality* as a transient 'accomplishment' of the actor. The citizens think that personality is activity which is rational, performance of any sanctioned action with clear awareness of what one is doing. (Here is a transparent conversion: taking misconduct to be motivated breaking of sanctions, the one-time-offender claims that he supports sanctions, his offense was unmotivated, an action "unlike himself", and therefore unreal, something for which he cannot be held responsible.) Rats confuse command-action with 'personality'. He who commands is a person, obeyers are animals. However, the criminal is not as vulgar as the advertiser. He wishes to be conspicuous (in a favorable sense) and to be obeyed. Instead of placing faith in a new suit or a more expensive car, he carries a gun. The gun is an equalizer, the only one available in present-day street life...

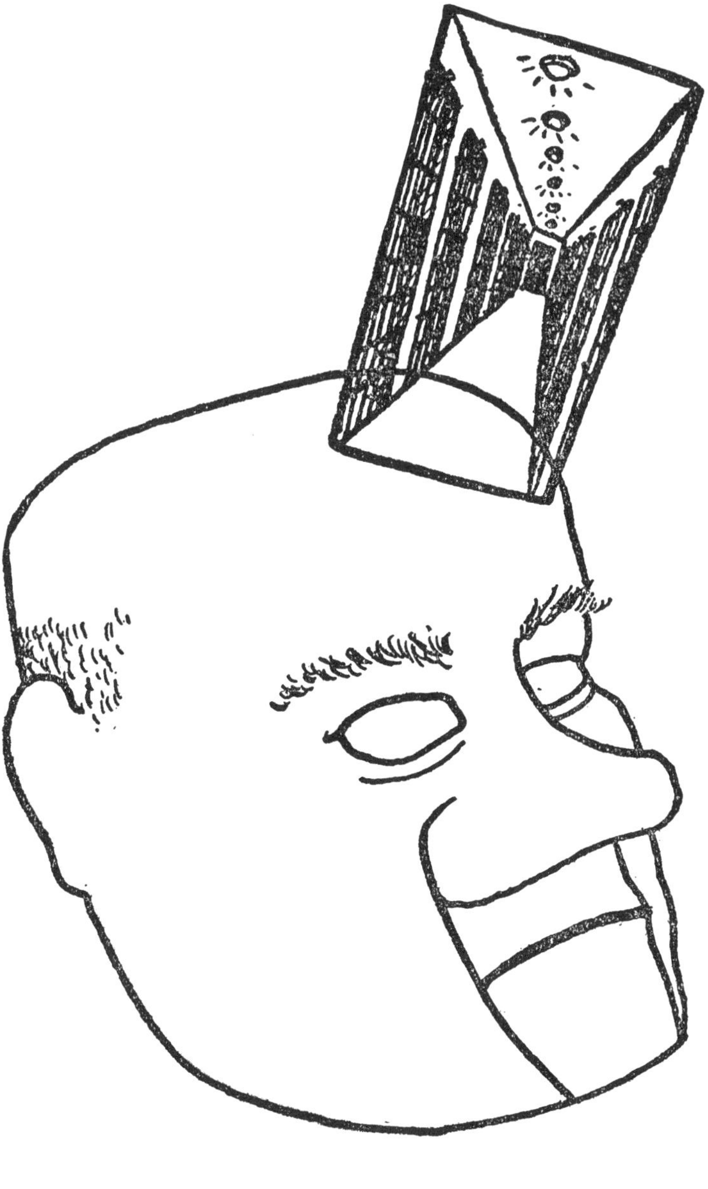

SECTION THREE

ARTS AND LETTERS

THE PRISON THEATRE

ROY FRANKLYN

Theatre is a group enterprise and perhaps its most vital component is the audience for which it performs. Of all theatres, those on Broadway and off, the Prison Theatre alone can relax in its knowledge of an assured audience for all its productions, regardless of what is being presented or what has gone before. Prison, in a sense, is a compact cosmos, and within its walls are men of divergent creeds, races, religions, political faiths, and educational backgrounds. Yet for each theatrical attraction presented, the majority of these men will leave their cells or dormitories, march in lines to sit on uncomfortable chairs on an unsloped floor for a few hours and witness any show regardless of its quality. The Prison Theatre is their escape from the deadly monotony of a uniform, regulated existence; it is their grasp for the reality of the "outside" world. The event becomes one of the main topics of conversation during the week, making it a social obligation for one to see the productions so as not to be at a loss in group bull-sessions.

Social pressure is an acute force in prison. (If one were ever in a performance and then had to live intimately with each and every member of the audience, he would immediately recognize the truth of this statement.) It is social pressure that regulates the quality of the productions, the first performance of the season being accepted as the norm. From then on, any show above norm is received with praise, while any show falling below the norm is treated to quantities of talk, both during and after the performance.

Many prisons attempt but few theatrical enterprises aside from the regularly scheduled Saturday nite movie, and these few attractions are usually of a musical-vaudeville stereotype which allows the maximum of inmates to participate with the least amount of energy for all concerned. Such a variety show usually consists of one or two piano players, perhaps one specialty dancer, several potential Crosbys, a fellow who makes a rhythmic clatter with a pair of ordinary tablespoons, and, if the group is really ambitious, perhaps the Prison Orchestra, all being introduced by a master of ceremonies who performs his usual function of occassionally telling a joke which inevitably falls flat. Perhaps a skit or two (the acting out of one of the master of ceremonies' jokes) might be included, but if this is done, the production is usually heralded for months in advance as "The Winter Show", the major production of the season. In short, there is little that is creative in the theatre, little that is more than the Usual, the Expected.

The potentialities for an imaginative theatre within the particular prison walls behind which I found myself confined seemed waiting to be called forth. The Prison Administration of the institution was somewhat cooperative, the audience, due to the quantity of technical violators of war-time regulations, approached a metropolitan level of educational background, and there was a small group with talent and eagerness to be exploited.

Our season had begun with a series of community nites each Sunday which presented the usual form of variety show. Behind us was the experience of the one attempt at seriousness on the stage, our unsuccessful Christmas Show which had included a choral group, a solo singer of carols, and readings of appropriate selections woven into a whole by discriminate lighting effects.

Unfortunately, we had announced it merely as a "Christmas Show," and when the curtains opened on all the solemnity, the audience, accustomed to more raucous forms, felt unjustly "taken in". As those who wished to leave couldn't—(prison rules do not allow one to leave until the end of the show)—they proceeded noisily to give their opinion of the apparent hoax by crumbling paper, stamping feet, and intermittent loud comments done in underground fashion so that the guards, who acted as tyrannical ushers, could not spot the disturbance.

Our failure was analyzed by ourselves as being caused by faulty advertising and it was thru this production that we recognized the value of advertising the performances by placing attractively mimeographed notices on various bulletin boards. The advertising became as important a factor in the appreciaton of the performance as the quality of the show itself, for it provided the audience with a common expectation before the rise of the curtain, a quality usually lacking in prison audiences, and also gave them a larger sense of choice as to whether or not they should view the show. No doubt this larger sense of choice was very flattering, for choice is a rare thing in prison where life is regulated for you by toy whistles and toy badges, and it was because of this sense of choice that but few of the regular audience refused to attend our next all-serious attempt. We advertised it as "Strictly for Long-Hairs", subtitled it "An Experimental Concert", and boasted a Beethoven sonata for violin and piano, some Debussy and several concert songs, all by our own inmate talent. The audience was generous in applause and this time there was no commotion in the auditorium, even during the long musical passages which can be quite boring to one not musically interested. We pronounced our experiment a success.

Meanwhile being committed to a show every other week we tried our best to add just a little imagination to the inevitable variety show. Once we presented a mock radio show which supposedly was sponsored by the makers of the low grade tobacco the Bureau of Prisons provided for our use. Into this form we were able to voice our protests against the petty irritations of prison routine, all subtly written so as not to arouse censorship, but not too subtle in its presentation to pass over the heads of the audience. They picked up their cues and responded genially; in fact, the officer who was directly answerable for the show began to wonder if it was wise to allow us, the producers, free rein. But as the number of inmates attending rose slightly after each production (which made his reports look better when he sent them to Washington), he did not noticeably interfere.

At first we were reluctant to tempt fate a second time with another all-serious attempt, but the compelling enthusiasm of our leading—and only—concert singer for some form of presentation of the opera "Pagliacci" at last prevailed and this became our crowning success and with it we closed our season. We finally evolved a orm in relation to available talent, and announced our plans for the opera "Pagliacci, Arranged in Dramatic Form for a Singer, a Narrator, and a Pianist". Our largest difficulty in the actual work of producing the show, aside from the plethora of rules limiting our availability for rehearsals, was the prison auditorium with its bare stage and minimum lighting equipment. (Prison auditoriums are usually bad examples of architecture, being designed as all-purpose auditoriums, and thus serving no one purpose well.)

The guard under whom we worked, our titular boss, at last tried to assert himself. He began to worry about the attendance figures and asked us not to stress the word "opera" in our announcements. But we were adamant, believing the audience should know beforehand exactly what to expect. However he did insist that our presentation be preceded by the so-called "Educational Movies", which were quite popular with the inmates, films distributed by industrial firms explaining their processes of manufacturing. We submitted to this proposal only after he guaranteed that, for that one nite, prison rules would be changed and the doors would be unlocked after the film showing to allow those not interested in our opera to go back to their cells and dormitories. Actually, this was a great concession on his part as it is often easier "for a camel to thread the postern of a needle's eye" than to change the sacred prison rules. The nite of the performance arrived and an unusually large audience attended. After the film showing the doors were unlocked and we waited to see how many would remain in their seats. Only three persons went back to their quarters. We heaved a sigh of relief and shot a triumphant glance at the guard, but he was busy speaking to the other guards and acting as if the entire affair had been his idea. Then the doors were relocked, our house-lites clicked off, and the pianist started the overture to the Prison Theatre's production of "Pagliacci". From then on, the audience was ours. As the final curtain fell, the audience was enthusiastic in its acclamation and hailed the production as the culmination of our efforts towards a better theatre. A creative theatre, lacking in so many places in the world, had found an appreciative audience behind prison walls.

ARTHUR KASSIN

BEHEST OF THE GOVERNMENT

Is it a jest of the government
That I'm fed and dressed by the government,
Repressed and suppressed by the government,
Distressed and depressed by the government?

And when I protest to the government
That I'm oppressed by the government,
Why is it stressed by the government—
That I am a "guest of the government"?

A CELEBRITY

I'm rather ordinary,
And fame can pass me by;
I cannot act distinguished,
Nor will I ever try.

If I must be outstanding,
(A thing I've never been)
Renown enough if I could be
Outstanding looking in.

Let others strive for honors,
I've got a simple goal:
I'd like to be remembered
As one who made parole.

KASSIN

JUDGMENT

One judge
Had sentenced his erring fellow-mortal
To "Death";
The other judger of men
(Hailed for his magnanimity)
Had sentenced his victim
To "Life".
The fantastic world of difference
Between the two judgments:
One,
A quick painless cessation of life—
"Death";
The other,
A thousand tormented deaths—
"Life".
And, in between, lay snuggled
The dreamless untroubled sleep of both judges—
"Reality".

MUSIC AND PRISON BARS

Music fills my head with fancies—
Our mud enclosure is no more;
But when the notes merge into silence,
The walls are closer than before.

KASSIN

GRASPING AT THE LAST STRAW

You admonish us
Not to step on the grass,
And we're touched by your concern
For the vegetation,
Can it be that, indeed,
You have a sense of beauty?
Or are you merely following the directions
To be found in some book of regulations?
If, perchance, the growth of grass
Stirs something fine within you,
Who knows—
You might even be inclined
To cease trampling our spirits;
And our hearts, once fertile
And productive,
But long barren
From lack of nourishment
Derived through understanding,
Might once again quicken
With hopes—
Of justice.

HAIR RAZING TALE

The mustache I grew in the month of July
Was never intended to harm man or beast...
For defacing the government's property—
My mustache was cut and my sentence increased!

JAMES HOLMES

from POEMS FROM PRISON

Prison's a probing pain
that moods my mind,
that deads my deeds and leaves, lowly, behind
soul slaked, empty, insane.
Freedom can better be
but brunter to bear,
born of the sloughed off self, the left lair,
and the open hunger for thee.

Ungird me, god, this gear
that heavies my heart;
mend my lewd loves, my hates, made-at-mart,
cheap-bought, cherished, dear.
I would desire to be
in barren bliss,
my soul seared of all other things but this—
living longing for thee.

E. R. KARR

SONNET OF A WAR OBJECTOR

On hearing Beethoven where steel and stone
Absorb no particle of sound, the fault
Is little and is easy to condone.
Enough that music fills this stone-steel vault,
Enlivens with the effervescent Eighth
The spirit caged in body that is caged.
Play on, sweet sound, the magic on your breath
Has touched the buried soul before, assuaged
The troubles of this unpitied planet Earth.
When all about me is a raucous rave
That kills the minds of men, you bring rebirth
Where otherwise would be the living grave.
    Except for you would perish all I've dreamed;
    In you humanity has been redeemed.

Written after two years in UPPER HARTFORD
CELL HOUSE, DANBURY FED. PRISON

            To me the prison feels like a place way up high, with sheer perpendicular cliffs descending on all sides......I imagine that no greenery grows for miles around the place, that the surrounding countryside is nothing but a field of huge, jagged, broken boulders very difficult to pass through. I imagine if I were out among the boulders I'd find those closest to the cliffs to be the sharpest and largest. Out a few miles from the prison, I'd expect to find smaller boulders and stones. Then as I got further away, the stones would become smaller and smaller, smoother. If I were out among the stones the further I got away from the prison the easier the travel would be.

            If I could get to one of the prison's outside windows, and look out, I imagine I would be able to see the greenery begin just beyond the field of broken stones. It would be barely visible, all around, just on the horizon!

                                    LOWELL NAEVE

MADE-WORK

STURGE STEINERT

Three of them were loading the truck.

The other three were standing around leaning on their shovels, stamping their feet occasionally in a desultory attempt to keep warm.

The guard stood mutely by with a stupid stare—he looked uncomfortable.

Gravel and dirt hit the bed of the truck in slow, monotonous rhythm.

About half a mile down the road a car came to the crest of a small rise.

The guard was alerted and tense.

"Okay, you guys; get busy, here comes the warden."

Two of the idle three shuffled to the truck; their long-handled shovels were swung to the pile. The others moved a bit. Even with alternate throws their shovels banged, the handles thudded as they loaded.

The warden's car turned slowly into the intersection.

"Morning, Grimes", he said to the hack.

Officer Grimes acknowledged his greeting with a stiff bow, half salute and mumbled salutation.

The warden noticed the man leaning on his shovel.

"Hey Mathews, come here".

Mathews looked uninterested, dropped his shovel and walked toward the car.

"Yes sir?" he queried.

"Why aren't you working, Mathews?"

"I am working, sir."

"You were leaning on your shovel and the others were loading. Is that your conception of work?"

Looking very patient, Mathews explained.

"Well, three of us were leaning on our shovels until your car came in sight, sir, and then Mr. Grimes ordered us all to get busy. You see we load in shifts of three because there isn't room for all of us to load at once."

The warden grunted "muguwughapft...v," released the clutch pedal and sped up the hill toward the prison.

The hack had heard everything; his face looked like a putty mask. It was a baby's face and usually had bright red cheeks, yellow eyebrows and wide blue eyes. A turtle neck sweater with a big "Y" and a tennis racket instead of a pistol would have looked more natural.

"Mathews," he commanded, "Come here."

"Yes sir?"

"Dig a hole right here about four feet long and three feet wide and dig it as deep as you like."

"What for, sir?"

"Because I said so," snapped Grimes.

Mathews thought a moment and then, "What are you going to do with it, sir?"

The hack tried to look fiendish but only succeeded in looking silly, "I'm going to have you fill it up again."

"I won't do it" Mathews said.

"You're refusing to work?" Grimes sounded incredulous.

"No sir, I'm not refusing to work; what you told me to do isn't work." Mathews seemed to come alive. "There's plenty of work to be done without doing made work! Hell, Mr. Grimes, I won't do made work even if I'm paid."

They hadn't noticed the lieutenant's car until it was on top of them. He rolled down the window and saluted Grimes pleasantly with "How's everything?"

Grimes turned to the car; he said gleefully, "Number 336 refuses to work! Will you take him back, Lieutenant Masterson?"

"You mean Mathews?" The lieutenant had just a hint of sarcasm in his question. "What's it all about, Mathews?"

"I said he refused to work." Grimes was peeved.

"Get, in Mathews." Masterson opened the door and without another word drove back to the prison.

Bart Mathews was sitting in the isolation cell waiting further action. There wasn't much else to do but sit since the cell contained only a bed, chair and toilet. He supposed that they would bring him before the "board" for a hearing.

He had often joked about this board to his fellow prisoners. He called it the inquisition. Of all the cases the board had heard no one had ever been declared innocent of the charges brought against them. Someone had raised the question of why they (the prison authorities) bothered having a board at all. Bart's explanation was that it must be either of two reasons: one, that Congress in its infinite wisdom had decided to liberalize the prison system, or, two, that the Department of Justice wanted to prevent an individual from being responsible in case the judgment of the board created a stink.

Bart was sick at heart. This was supposed to be a model prison, in fact it wasn't called a prison—it was a correctional institution. When Bart had been admitted the Warden had had a little talk with him and explained, "We do not mean to punish you. There is no room for vengeance in the penal code. What we seek to do is rehabilitate men so that they can fit into the social mold."

Since then he had heard "rehabilitation" spoken of so often and with such reverance he felt that some major cult was growing around the idea with the warden as high priest.

The cell door was opened. A hack said, "Come on, you."

They entered the Captain's office and there was the board. The Captain—he was the Department of Mass Treatment; the Warden—the Department of Individual Treatment; the doctor—a would-be psychiatrist who was always looking for broken homes in the earlier life of the prisoners; the Assistant Warden—the Warden's call boy who had majored in Sociology. He was scientific in his approach and to him a slide rule was a phallus. And the Senior Lieutenant—he was contact man with the masses.

The Captain conducted the hearing. He was very grave, very military and hell-bent for an end to this nonsense. He got down to business immediately and ordered Grimes to present the charge.

Grimes: "It's simple enough—Mathews refused to work. You knew how difficult he is; he's just a trouble-maker. He acts as if the prison...ah, institution, were a fraternity house and just decided not to work".

The Captain: "Well, Mathews?"

Mathews looked at the iron faces in front of him: "Mr. Grimes distorts the thing com......"

"Give us the facts, Mathews. Don't make a speech about Grimes", interupted the Captain.

After a very obvious grimace Mathews started again. "Six of us were loading a truck in turns; three waiting and three shoveling. The Warden's car came in sight..."

The Captain stopped him, "Is this pertinent, Mr. Grimes? Does this have any bearing on the case?"

"No sir," said Grimes. "All that happened was I ordered Number 336 to dig a hole and he refused to do it."

Bart appealed to the Warden with his eyes; the Warden looked right through him.

"Well Mathews, what do you say to this?" The Captain

was in a hurry.

"I have to give you all the facts, Captain," Mathews started again. "Now when the Ward..."

"Did you refuse to dig the hole?" shouted the Captain.

"But Captain..."

"Did you?" he banged the table this time.

"YES" Bart screamed.

The Captain looked relieved. "I'm through" anyone else want to question him?"

Bart was furious; he leaped up shouting "Grimes is yellow! he ordered me to do made work because he's afraid of the Warden. He wanted me to dig a hole and fill it up..."

That was ao far as he got. The Captain was bellowing: "Shut up!—SHUT HIM UP!"

All the rest were on their feet; the doctor and Assistant Warden advanced to restrain Mathews; Grimes had turned at least three colors and looked as if he had been hit in the face. Things quieted suddenly.

The Captain was livid. "We try to be fair, we want to give you a hearing; and you scream insults at the officers. What you have done is enough to have you thrown in the hole. This is..."

The Warden had gestured. The Captain stopped; everyone looked grave, "Mathews, your attitude is outrageous; you are like a spoiled child. Can't you be a little dignified? Don't you have any respect for anyone? Now, answer this question: Will you do the work assigned to you?"

"That depends..."

"Answer, YES or NO!"

"I won't do made work."

The Warden simpered, "Always have to have the last word, Don't you. Well the answer is no."

With that the Warden signed off and started to look at nothing again. The doctor leaned foward and signaled for attention. The Captain nodded.

The doctor was almost rubbing his hands. He purred, "Now,

Mathews, why do you persist on rebelling. What perverse streak in you leads you to do these things. Was there something in the past that made you be so distrustful, made you want to flaunt authority? Why, the very reason that you're here, refusing to register for the draft is so silly..." He was looking eager now.

Bart sat there almost snarling, "Ah, nuts," he said.

"You see", sighed the doctor, "completely uncooperative, a disciple of discontent. I fear there is nothing to be done at the moment, Captain, but I do recommend that he be instructed to visit me a couple of times a week...after he's out of isolation, of course."

Bart was convinced now, everything had been decided before he had walked in.

"Any more questions?" the Captain paused, "If not, remove the prisoner and we shall decide the case."

Bart was escorted to a bench in the hall by Grimes. Grimes also remained outside while the board pondered...a polite and superficial gesture toward democratic proceeding. Neither of them spoke. Bart's thoughts were leapfrogging through a reenactment of the farce; the hack was trying to determine whether he had come through the show with a mark of approval in the Warden's docket. He came to no conclusion, during the hearing the Warden had betrayed nothing except his distaste for Mathews...

Back in the office again.

Th Department of Individual Treatment was leaning forward; the Department of Mass Treatment imitating the great stone face; the doctor smiling coquettishly; the Assistant Warden striking the pose of his hero, and the Senior Lieutenant blurred with the background.

"Our decision," the Captain breathed each syllable, "is that you will be given a new work assignment...and thirty days in isolation."

Bart shrugged his way back to the cell. He was looking unruffled—you can't imagine thirty days isolation—you have to live it.

Masterson stopped by the cell later in the day. He offered Bart a cigarette.

"I heard about it, just got the details. You know, Mathews, I used to belong to a radical political party so I guess I can figure this. I got tired being kicked in the face and decided to do a little kicking. Now I play games with Washington..." he faded away.

Bart didn't take the lead; he was too preoccupied with the next thirty days.

The Warden was making hieroglyphics in a book. He muttered, "Damn Grimes! Our best pitcher stuck away for thirty days—the Lion's Club game next Sunday; now we haven't a chance." He stabbed the book with an ominous stroke.

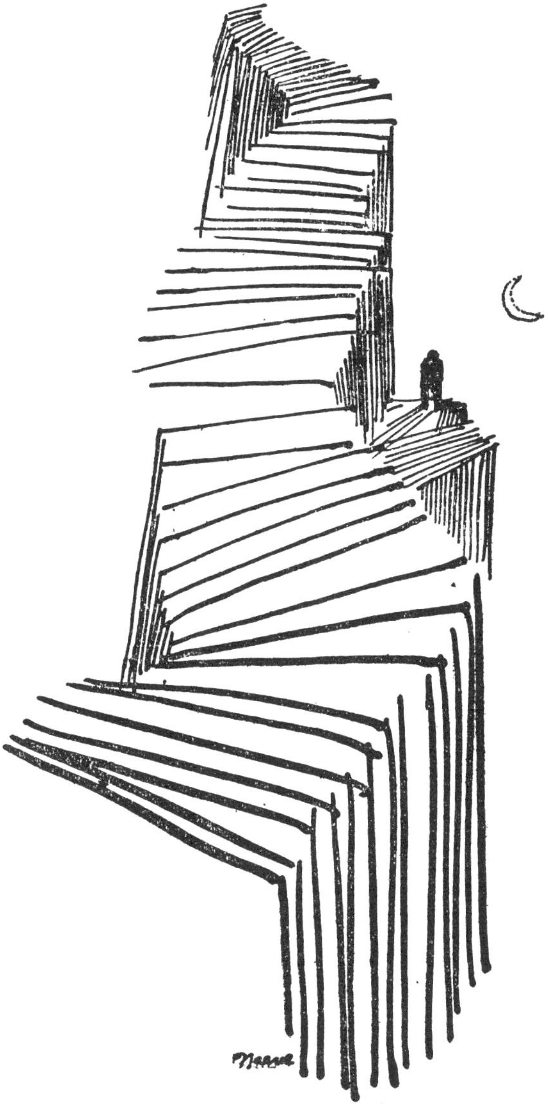

LETTER

Dear Mr. L——:

Your questionnaire on prisons has been with my unanswered mail for months. I have no enthusiasm for answering it. However, it is only fair to tell you that I think that answering such questionnaires, if it has any effect at all, does more harm than good.

A few simple facts about prison should make this clear:

1) *The system rests ultimately on authority* backed by the threat of death to those who attempt to escape, by the threat of solitary to those who do not conform, and by the day-by-day *fact* of insidious encroachments on every man's personality, whether he conforms or not.

The prisoner in the modern liberal and scientific institution has most of the same frustrations as the man in the old-style prison or modern county jail—but with this added disadvantage: he is now managed "scientifically" from some remote-control board to which he does not have access. No prisoner has any confidence that the immense amount of data which is collected on him will be used for his benefit. Most prisoners know that the subtle pressures constantly put upon them have nothing to do with their welfare but much to do with "prison security"—and with the job security of the penologist. The prisoner's need to live and the system's attempt to live for him (and off him) can never be reconciled.

2) *The justification of this system of authority rests upon a previous moral judgment of the man's action.* Almost as often as not this 'moral' judgment is based on a system of law which has little to do with any concept of ethics.

A man is convicted of 'conspiracy' because there is inadequate evidence that he actually committed an offense, or because he can be given an additional four or five years for 'conspiring' to steal a car on top of the sentence for stealing it. He is convicted of income tax evasion because conviction on charges of various racketeering activities would involve other people whom the government has no desire to prosecute. He is convicted under the Mann Act because his best girl fell in love with someone else. In the Army, he is convicted of mutiny because a young whelp of an officer pushed his men beyond human endurance. Or he is convicted of rape because some girl got panicky (or because his skin is black —and *anyone* knows that black men are rapists!) and he winds up with anything from twenty years to life. As a civilian in wartime, after volunteering several times for the Army and finally finding himself on the way to a tuberculosis sanitarium, he is picked up by the FBI and given three years for failure to notify his draft board of a change in address. Or as a refugee from the Franco regime and a French internment camp he gets a year and a day for illegal entry into what he had thought was a natural place to seek refuge—the United States.

I know little about the statistics of convictions, but I should say that a large number of convictions are as ethically questionable as these. But whether they are or not, the important point is that they are based on a *judgment*, in which the prisoner did not participate. He is in possession of a complicated set of subjective and objective facts which the judge did not, and to a large extent could not, take into consideration. He will probably either feel that the judge was completely unaware that these facts existed or that he was downright vicious. Consequently he will consider his view far superior to that of the judge, and with good reason. Prisoners understand many things that judges do not. And in the type of examples I have just given, even someone who is not a prisoner can understand.

As long as the sense of moral superiority which is implicit in *judgment* remains, the lawbreaker will be acutely aware of considerable moral superiority to the judge and jailer. And *any* prison program based on this defective judgment will seem to him particularly pointless. No effective treatment can be devised while the criminal law court remains.

3) *There can be no rapport between prisoner and jailer.* Jailers, or "custodial officers", are known to the men as "hacks" or "screws". A screw is a screw, the lowest of the low, a man you can't trust, a man with no self-respect, and a man with whom you'd better have nonhing to do. This is more than an emotional reaction. It is based on generations of experience, experience which the best of prison reform cannot wipe out. All human relations are contaminated by any caste system. Within the prison, the caste system is solidified. Fear of crossing the line is about as strong in the officers as in the men, although they are subject to different types of reprisals. Across this line of suspicion few creative thoughts can pass. There can be no man-to-man feelings. You can call a hack a custodial officer. You can require him to pass civil service examinations. You can offer enough pay to attract "qualified" men to the job. You can loosen up the institution from a "penitentiary" to a "correctional institution" or even to an "honor camp". There will be no *rapport*: A screw is still a screw. He is the agent who acts for the authority you reject on the basis of a moral judgment which is unsound in a program for which you have no stomach.

4) *The prison system is essentially window-dressing for a corrupt society.* It collects a few unfortunate individuals, makes a great show of "protecting society" by dealing out justice to them, adds to their misfortune, and turns them back into this same protected society as somewhat greater liabilities than before. Meanwhile the real criminals—if there are such things—run our big business, our government, and the outright rackets which operate on the fringes of both, unmolested. More than being unmolested, they

actively engage in throwing a few pseudo-criminals to the wolves. The prisons are for pseudo-criminals. I would not advocate locking up Henry Ford, Mayor Hague, Franklin Roosevelt, or Colonel McCormick. But for those who believe either in "protecting society" or "rehabilitating" men, such men as these, who happen to *be* a detriment to the lives of most of us, are much more logical choices.

From these facts I can only conclude that it is a waste of time to try to devise better methods for coercing the small-fry thieves and murderers, the amoral victims of legal red tape, and the innocent victims of police justice—coercing them into some kind of conformity with a political and economic system which operates for the good of a few and against the best interest of the majority. And what is a better system to be used for but to perpetuate the conditions that send men to prison?

There is no "better" prison system. Nothing will do the trick except abolition. I should hate to be accused of dreaming that this will happen in a vacuum—like wishing that the National City Bank might be socialized, irrespective of the rest of the economy. Nevertheless, I want the National City Bank taken over, and the prisons abolished and I am only incidentally interested in lower interest rates and fewer prison restrictions. Studies pointed toward liberalization only impede breaking down the myth that prisons have to stay.

From this I hope it is clear why I don't fill out your questionaire. What difference does it make what were the traits of a custodial officer? Custodial officers cannot be judged by traits. What interpretation can you possibly put on my telling "what was most commendable" about custodial officers, when I say that the only commendable thing was their tendency, once in a while, to act as humans and to fail to enforce the rules of the institution?

Since I am not filling out your questionaire, I may as well state as a minimum fact justifying this tirade that I did two years in the Federal Penitentiary at Lewisburg, Pennsylvania, for violation of the Selective Service and Training Act. During the short time that I was there the Federal Bureau of Prisons collected an immense "jacket" of information about me—some of it, I presume, completely untrue, much of it badly interpreted, and perhaps some of it true and even intelligent analysis. None of it will be used in helping me to adjust myself to this society—assuming that that is a good idea. It certainly will not be used in adjusting our society to me, to my fellow criminals on whom they have similar jackets, and to the millions of others in this country who are as badly in need of better economic and political conditions.

If you want to understand the prison system I suggest that you go out and commit a "crime"—something like robbing a bank, which might be a commendable thing to do from a moral standpoint, and to which there is attached a fairly strong stigma. Thus you wouldn't miss the full flavor of the experience of going through the courts and the prison. Some day, perhaps, we'll commit this "crime" collectively, and then it will not be a crime. And if we're intelligent enough, we'll begin to realize that there are no crimes, and no need to maintain institutions for treating men as criminals.

In the meantime you might try to emancipate the criminologists themselves. They will be emancipated when they cease being criminologists—when they are no longer the paid servants of the ruling classes, and when they regard men not as cases but as equals. You don't have to throw all psychology overboard in order to treat a man as an equal. But you have to give up having him hauled into your office by a policeman, sitting him in a chair—even an easy chair—for an interview, and giving him any other impression than this: that you're going to work this thing out together. You can be just as damned hostle as you like—I don't care—but try to have a little respect for the man! He will have little enough respect for you.

You have my best wishes that you'll turn up something of value. I do think, though, that you ought to rob a bank.

          Sincerely,
          WILLIAM H. KUENNING

LETTER

Dear Friends,

I meant to reply to your note requesting an article for the prison book sooner. I have quite a mass of material here, but it has never been co-ordinated properly or written up. One reason is that I am not especially gifted as a writer, and feel that I could not adequately express some of the more important and frequently overlooked effects of imprisonment on the personality. Another reason is that I have come to strong disagreement with many of the tactics used by CO's in prison to impress the public—i.e. work and hunger strikes against censorship, jimcrow,etc.—and even now feel that the basic issue is individual evasion of service to the state and not what public opinion considers "conscientious."

The most genuine protests were those directed against imprisonment itself (and the whole coercive apparatus of which prisons are a part). My own observation convinces me that these protests are constantly being made by inconspicuous prisoners branded as "criminals" who have no civil liberty groups or clergymen to publicize their feelings, and who, accordingly, bring upon themselves the full measure of psychological and sometimes physical sadism which the state has devised to serve its ends. Inadequate and irresponsible as such protests may be, in contrast to the COs' planned actions, carefully toned down so as not to offend certain sections of public opinion, they do reflect a craving for some kind of freedom which, in many cases, is not even expressed in positive terms. The capitalization of 'honesty', 'sincerity' etc., has tended to alienate me from the majority of CO's.

In regard to the Springfield institution, where the bulk of my time was spent, I feel that the wide publicity given to physical brutalities (while good) has tended to make people overlook the less sensational but far more important rôle of this prison—beating down all resistance and crushing all individuality. Where the state does not succeed in making an obedient lackey, at least it does reduce the individual to something less than human—an automaton cowed into submission. Springfield is called upon to perform the latter function where other federal prisons fail in the first, and, I regret to say, it does an excellent job. Detailed analysis of the various mechanisms used to perform this function is the sort of material on Springfield which should be published widely.

I have been very disgusted also by the 'iron curtain' erected by most CO publicity groups in regard to discussion of sex life in prison. While this phase must be considered in relation to the whole idea of imprisonment, those analyses which have carefully avoided any mention of the subject have been inadequate. Of course Springfield had the distinction of housing all the sex perverts among the federal prison population (CPI no. 3), but in reality transfers were made only when expedient to the administration and some form of sex outlet was provided by the inmates at all other prisons and jails (about 15) I stayed in prior to my time in Springfield....

Sincerely
JACK HEWELIKE